CRAFTS OF CHINA

CRAFTS OF
THE WORLD

CRAFTS OF
CHINA

Michael Carter

DOUBLEDAY AND COMPANY, INC.
GARDEN CITY, NEW YORK, 1977

This book was conceived and produced
by Martensson Books London

EXECUTIVE EDITOR   Wendy Martensson

CRAFTS EDITOR   Pamela Tubby

ASSOCIATE EDITOR   Alice Beale

RESEARCH   Ron Davis

PICTURE RESEARCH   Penny Brown
                     Patricia Mandel

PHOTOGRAPHY   Chris Overton

DESIGN   Flax + Kingsnorth

ILLUSTRATORS   Marion Appleton
                     Farhana Khan
                     Flax + Kingsnorth
                     Paul Williams

TECHNICAL ADVISORS   Gillian Higham
                     Alf Martensson
                     Erland Russell

The publishers would like to thank
Mary Penn of the Sino-British Trade
Council for her invaluable help in the
early days of this book, and the
Commercial Office of the Embassy of
the People's Republic of China for
their assistance on the project.

Thanks are also due to Liberty's of
London, The Neal Street Shop and Mr.
and Mrs. Colin Penn for supplying
Chinese items to be photographed, to
Marguerite Fawdry and Pollock's Toy
Museum for lending essential research
material, and to David Pelham for
his kind assistance.

Doubleday and Company
ISBN: 0-385-13119-4
Library of Congress Catalog
Card No. 76-51862
© 1977 Aldus Books Limited, London
Printed and bound in Italy by
Amilcare Pizzi S.p.A.
Cinisello Balsamo (Milano)

CONTENTS

CHAPTER 1
THE BLOSSOMING OF A HUNDRED FLOWERS

Dragon motifs from part of a door decoration in the Imperial Palace in Peking.

Opposite: China old and new: a grandmother and child at Sha Chiao commune near Kwangchow.

Around the two great rivers of China, the Yangtze and the Yellow River, are formed two vast, fertile plains that from ancient times have been the heart of Chinese civilization. To the north of these plains lie the hostile and barren Mongolian Steppes, while to the west they are bordered by the mountains of Tibet. In southern China, tropical swamps gradually give way to the dense jungles of the Southeast Asian peninsula and to the east the great plains meet the sea. It is not surprising, then, that the Chinese rarely use the name China for their country. Instead they call it *chung kuo* or "the Central Country," a name more appropriate to this vast nation, bounded on all sides by inhospitable lands.

The origin of Chinese culture is cloaked in mystery, and scholars argue about its source. There is a Chinese legend that tells of the beginning of the universe and of man which goes far in explaining the multitude of forms and motifs that fill the work of their craftsmen. From all eternity, it is said, there was the Tao, which eventually became the Great Monad or *T'ai-chi*. The Great Monad separated into Yang, the positive principle of Light, Heaven, Sun and Vigor, and Yin, the negative principle of Darkness, Earth, Moon and Quiescence. In Chinese symbolism Yin and Yang are shown as a swirling "S" in black and white, set within a circle representing an egg. In the legend, the egg then hatched and P'an Ku, the Chinese Adam emerged from the egg. One half of it remained above him and the other below, gradually becoming more separated as P'an Ku grew. For 18,000 years he continued to grow, all the while chiseling out the universe and at the end of this time he collapsed and died. The remains of his body are believed to have formed the details of nature as we see it. His head became the mountains, his blood the rivers. The sun and moon were formed from his two eyes, and the soil from his flesh, while his skin and hair became the trees and plants, his

Lavish decoration embellishes the Imperial Palace in Peking, once the secluded home of Emperors, now open to all the people.

marrow became pearls and precious stones. Man was formed from the parasites on his body. The wind we hear is his breath, and the thunder is his voice.

With man so intimately associated with nature it is not surprising that the early Chinese believed that all matter, whether animate or inanimate, possessed an independent spirit. Some of these spirits were believed to be those of dead ancestors who looked after the living, and all spirits were believed to influence the affairs of men.

Many of the earliest motifs used by craftsmen were of the animals, both real and imaginary, that had been chosen as the guardians of the world, protecting men from the spirit forces of nature. Foremost of these were the Four Beasts of the Quadrants. The East was guarded by the Dragon of Spring and signified the beginning of life, the South was protected by the Phoenix of Summer which was the zenith of life. The White Tiger of Autumn, symbolic of the time of the harvest and death, guarded the West and the Tortoise of Winter, which represented the time of hibernation, protected the North. From their origin, thousands of years ago the central significance of

The Summer Palace in Peking, built by the Dowager Empress in the early nineteenth century, is today a public recreation area.

these symbols remained unchanged, though they have taken on new meanings. The Dragon became the symbol of the Emperors, who were seen as the givers of life and the guardians of the people. Their Empresses took the Phoenix as their emblem. These symbolic guardians formed the basis of a multitude of Chinese motifs.

Yet the craftsman's concern with placing these guardians on his work, whether it was pottery, embroidery or carving did not continue. For, sometime in the first century B.C., he began to open his eyes and look at the world around him, at the landscapes, the flowers and the plants. This was the time of Confucius, whose philosophy was to influence 2000 years of Chinese society, and of his contemporary, Lao Tzu, the founder of Taoism whose ideal was communion with nature. Until the arrival of Buddhism in the first century A.D. it was Taoism that taught the artist and the craftsman

A decorated roof in Yangsu village near Kweilin.

Workers relax in the Summer Palace and enjoy its delightful water gardens.

Workers at Hangchow West Lake
harvest lotus leaves to be used as
packaging.

the beauty of the world around him. The Taoist idea of paradise is
filled with scenes that are still embroidered in silk, carved in jade and
lacquer and freely painted on porcelain. It is a region of bliss, with
towering, misty crags, with lakes, streams, bridges, pagodas, willow,
pine and peach trees. Floating in the sky are the Taoist gods and
beautiful birds. Birds are a favorite theme of the craftsman for they
symbolized the free, wandering spirit.

Buddhism arrived from India, during Han times, but did not
become fully established in China for another 500 years until the
T'ang Dynasty. Three hundred years later, by the time of the Sung
Dynasty, the influence of Buddhism, Taoism and primitive Chinese
beliefs about the world had combined to inspire in the craftsman a

An airy tracery of bamboo poles in a
field near Kwangchow.

level of perfection in form and design that many believe has not been equaled since. The Buddhist love of all living things completed the craftsman's catalogue of symbolic motifs. Flowers and plants in particular gained a lasting place in the craftsman's repertoire at this time. The pine, because of its long life, became a symbol of longevity; the bamboo represented bending before life's troubles; the peony was the flower of spring and joy, the chrysanthemum, the flower of autumn and joviality, and the wild plum stood against the harshness of winter. The lotus became the supreme flower as a symbol of purity and creative power.

The religious symbols of Buddhism, demons, devils, gate gods and angels also appear as craft motifs at this time. By the nineteenth century, the craftsman was filling his work with the innumerable designs available to him, often crowding as many as he could into one piece, a task which required more and more refined techniques.

It is curious that despite the beauty and refinement found in Chinese crafts, only the work itself is remembered and rarely is the name of the craftsman revealed or recorded on his work except in painting or calligraphy. Until the time of the first republic in 1912, craftsmen either worked for themselves or in one of the Imperial factories, which were devoted to producing the best of a particular craft for the Emperor and his court. In the nineteenth century, these workshops began to produce crafts to be sold abroad. It was in these factories or workshops that many of the crafts techniques were developed and refined. Unlike the private craftsman who depended for his living on the quantity of work he could produce, the Imperial craftsmen were given all the time they needed to produce the perfect work worthy of the court.

A long and arduous apprenticeship was required in order to gain admittance to the Imperial workshops, as well as a quality of workmanship that would bring the craftsman to the attention of the workshop officials, who scoured China seeking new talent.

Symbol of the Emperors, the five-clawed dragon in eternal pursuit of the sacred pearl decorates a wall in the Imperial Palace.

Making a purchase at the commune store at Shi Ma near Shichiachuang outside Peking.

By the nineteenth century and into the early years of this century, however, the private craftsman came into his own again with the arrival of foreigners from the West who were eager to buy exotic wares from China. Whole streets in Peking, Shanghai and Canton, now called Kwangchow, became devoted to a single craft and were named to indicate the specific activity that went on, for example, the Jade Market, the Street of Ivory and the Street of Lanterns. The private craftsman remained a poor man for the most part. The ivory carver had to make chopsticks to earn his living and could devote only his leisure hours to producing really fine examples of his craft, which he could then sell to foreign buyers. These carvings, which were often a figure of his favorite god or a fantastically carved landscape, took several years to complete. Because of the superstitious value attributed to jade, the jade carver had to carve little amulets and pendants to make his living. In a corner of his workshop, however, he would try to find time to carve a single piece which he felt was worthy of the mystical properties of the stone.

Not all craftsmen worked with materials that required months or years of work to complete. There were craftsmen who fashioned

Row upon row of their gleaming handiwork surrounds workers at the Foochow Bodiless Lacquerware factory as they check the finished products.

Children with painted cheeks perform a mime especially for visitors to their kindergarten.

paper and straw and bamboo into festive items used as decorations and for holidays. The Chinese calendar was once full of festivals commemorating the seasons of the year, the gods, the legends and their ancestors. Full of symbolism and ritual, these occasions called for more fleeting handicrafts: kites, lanterns, paper cuts and toys. For each occasion there was a particular lantern; the front-door lantern, the escorting lantern, the wedding lantern and the festival lantern. Fans, too, came in many styles depending on the season of the year and the fashion of the moment. These bright and festive crafts brought color and gaiety to everyday life in China.

Since the Revolution of 1949, the life of the craftsman has undergone many changes. The preceeding thirty-five years had seen a gradual decline in the standards of craftsmanship, particularly of the more skilled crafts such as jade, ivory and wood carving and cloisonné. This was due at least in part to a need to cater to a large export market whose buyers could not wait the necessarily lengthy period of time required to make crafts of quality. Also many craftsmen, at the request of their foreign buyers, were applying their skills to Western motifs and forms. The Chinese craftsman has always been highly adept at incorporating outside influences into his traditional motifs. For the most part, however, the inclusion of Western designs did little to enhance or advance the unique aesthetic qualities of Chinese crafts. Slowly the quality was declining and the traditional sense of balance and design was being forgotten. At the same time though, many craftsmen earned a good living from their work.

The hot springs near Sian are now a public recreation park and a popular spot for family outings.

In the early 1950s the government of the new People's Republic of China began to make attempts to rectify this sad state of affairs. Special craft centers were established, which now include the Peking Jade Studios, the Soochow Embroidery Research Institute, the Fukien Arts and Crafts Center and other centers in Shanghai, Shantung, Hupeh and Tientsin. The purpose of these centers is not only to produce crafts for home and export but also to serve as training schools and research institutes to study the history and techniques

Fields in Chekiang Province nourish young rice seedlings until they are ready for transplanting.

of native crafts and to create new crafts, methods and designs. The government gathered together many of the old craftsmen in these centers and gave them the responsibility of passing on their skills to young apprentices. In 1960 the Hangchow Handicraft School was opened and began to train students in wood and stone carving and basketwork. The training course lasts four years and students spend part of each year doing manual labor in addition to pursuing their studies. The retired craftsmen of Hangchow who still wish to work, have benches at the Research Institute for Applied Arts where they come and go as they please, give advice to students and perhaps work on one special project that they have not previously had time to make. Similar handicraft schools have now opened in Shanghai and Soochow, and from them, graduates go out to work in the handicraft workshops and craft centers all over the country.

Above: A peasant print of work in a textile factory. Right: The garden of the former Dowager Empress at the Imperial Palace.

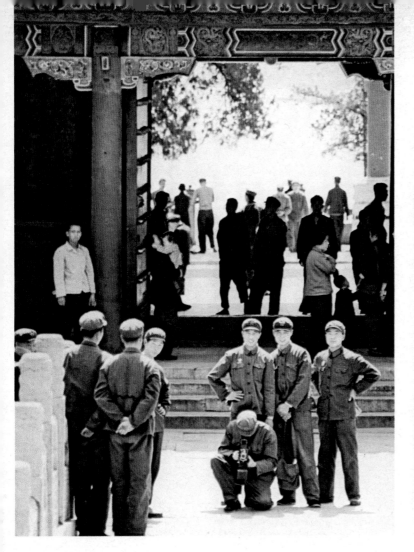

From the early years of new China, craftsmen have been encouraged to create modern and realistic designs depicting the workers and achievements of China. The Soochow Embroidery Research Institute has a group of textile designers and embroiderers who spend some time each year visiting the cities and rural areas observing the people and their accomplishments and then translating these into embroidery. The best known embroideries on these themes include the "Yangtze Bridge at Nanking," the "Red Flag Canal" and the work of a commune farming tangerines in Kiangsu Province called "A Bumper Crop of Tangerines."

Since the Cultural Revolution of the late 1960s, traditional Chinese designs and motifs have gradually become more popular again, particularly among crafts for export. The beauty and quality of Chinese crafts has been restored and sometimes even surpasses the best work of the previous three thousand years of Chinese craft history.

The craftsmen of China are again using their consummate skills to work with the old and experiment with the new, guided by Mao Tse-Tung's directives, "Let a hundred flowers blossom; weed through the old to let the new emerge" and "Make the past serve the present and foreign things serve China."

Soldiers on an outing pose for a souvenir picture at the Summer Palace in Peking.

A visit to the vegetable garden forms part of the day's activities for this kindergarten class.

**Major dynasties
of China**

Shang	1766–1122 B.C.
Chou	1122–249
Han	206 B.C.–220 A.D.
T'ang	618–906
Sung	960–1279
Ming	1368–1644
Ch'ing	1644–1912

•Urumchi

SINKIANG   UIGHUR

AUT.   REGION

T S I N G H A I

S Z E

TIBETAN AUT. REGION

•Lhasa

Kunmin

Y U N N A N

HEILUNGKIANG

REGION

AUT.

KIRIN

MONGOLIAN

LIAONING

Shenyang
(Mukden)

Kweisui

Tsunhwa

PEKING

Tientsin

Yinchwan   Hinghsien

NGSIA HUI
UT.

HOPEH

SHANSI

Yentai

SHANTUNG

Tsinan

Chengchow

Sian

HONAN

KIANGSU

SHENSI

ANHWEI

Hofei   Nanking

Wusih

Soochow

Shanghai

AN

HUPEH

Wuhan

Hangchow

CHEKIANG

Nanchang

Changsha

KIANGSI

HOW

HUNAN

iyang

Foochow

FUKIEN

KWANGSI
(CHUANG AUT. REGION)

KWANGTUNG

Kwangchow
(Canton)

Nanning

CHAPTER 2
CARVING THE RICHES OF THE EAST

Of the many natural materials that the Chinese craftsman has chosen to carve over the centuries, none has held so much fascination or possessed such magical qualities for him as jade. The Chinese word for jade is *yu*, meaning pure, precious and noble. Yet these are only some of the virtues ascribed to this stone. A classical Chinese book, the "Li Ki," tells us more.

> *Benevolence lies in its gleaming surface,*
> *Knowledge in its luminous qualities,*
> *Uprightness in its unyieldingness,*
> *Power in its harmlessness,*
> *Purity of soul in its rarity and spotlessness,*
> *Eternity in its durability. . . .*

The early Chinese believed that death was a long sleep from which one might, one day awaken. To protect the body during its sleep, relatives would place pieces of jade in the dead person's mouth. They believed that the stone contained the vital energy of the Yang principle which would triumph over the destructive Yin element contained in the soil. In this way they hoped that the body would not deteriorate.

Pao P'u-tzu, a Taoist philosopher of the fourth century, was reputed to have a secret drink which could give a man immortality. From the mountains where jade was found, he believed that a liquid flows, which, ten thousand years after appearing, turned to a solid, clear crystal. If this were mixed with a certain herb it became liquid again and a draft of this would confer the gift of living for a thousand years.

Not surprisingly, many of the first objects carved in jade were personal ornaments, for they were thought to have talismanic

A red and white jade belt buckle, a sacred Pi disk and a luminous jade medallion are just a few examples of fine Chinese carving.

Opposite: Liu Chi-Wu, a craftsman at the Peking Arts and Crafts Center, has been an ivory carver for over forty years.

In the final stages of carving jade the craftsman works with utmost care and concentration.

Right: A fine example of modern carving, this jade censer is produced for the export market.

properties. To wear a jade bracelet was to induce good health, though if the jade were to turn dull or break, then the wearer would meet with some misfortune. More sacred objects were also carved in jade. A perforated jade disk called a *pi* disk was the symbol of Heaven. It was believed to embody the light of the sun and provided a link with Heaven through its magical qualities. The Emperor, as the Son of Heaven, was able to consult with Heaven through the medium of the disk. There is still a prolific industry in these symbolic jades, particularly in Peking and Kwangchow, though the people of Mainland China do not, for the most part today, attribute to them the same superstitious values.

In pre-Revolution times, a main center of the jade trade was a large early morning, open-air market near the temple of the Five Hundred Disciples in what was then Canton. Here, both craftsmen and buyers would haggle for hours over the qualities of the various jades. The bargaining was not done out loud, however, particularly if another buyer was in the shop. Instead, seller and potential buyer would clasp each others' arms inside the baggy sleeves of their gowns and communicate by finger pressure. This way no one else would know the final price agreed.

The craftsman buying his piece of raw jade had to be especially discriminating in his choice, however, for he had to be able to judge from the crude stone what a finished piece would look like. A skilled craftsman can almost "see" inside the rough rock. He also has many different colors of jade to choose from. The term "jade" actually covers two kinds of stone – nephrite jade or true jade, and jadeite, which is regarded as a very good substitute. Both nephrite and jadeite come in a large variety of colors. The color of nephrite varies according to the amount of iron it contains, and is found in indigo, green, kingfisher blue, yellow, black and as a translucent colorless stone. Jadeite comes in over a hundred colors. According to Chinese folklore, red jade, known as *ch'iung*, was said to grow upon a huge tree which was found only in the palace gardens of Hsi Wang Mu, a Taoist fairy goddess, who lived in the mountains of K'un Lun. A particularly valued jade, called *hua hsueh tai tsao*, or "moss entangled in melting snow," is distinguished by streaks of green in a background of white.

Jade occurs naturally in deposits on the ground and in rivers. The former is found in large veins on the mountain slopes. Mining the veins used to be a very wasteful process. During the day charcoal fires would be lit along the veins. At night the fires would be put out, and the cold night air would crack the hot jade. In the morning, workmen would drive large wooden wedges into the cracks and break off the stone. A Manchu author has given us a colorful account of jade that is found in riverbeds. "There is a river in the territory of Yarkand in which is found jade pebbles. The largest are as big as round fruit dishes, the smallest the size of a fist or chestnut, and some of the boulders weigh more than five hundred pounds. There are many different colors . . . but the most difficult pieces to find are of pure mutton-fat texture with vermilion spots and others of bright spinach-green flecked with shining points of gold, so that these two varieties rank as the rarest and most precious of jades."

The variety of color, texture, grain and spots or veins of discoloration found in jade, are all important to the jade craftsman when

Months of work have gone into carving this tiny jade snuff bottle, which is surrounded with delicate fish and water-garden plants.

Master craftsmen in modern China keep the ancient skills alive by instructing young students in the art of carving.

21

The skill of the jade carver is in using the colors of the stone to best effect, as seen in this carving of a butterfly and lotus leaf.

he considers the best way in which to carve a particular piece. The true expert does not decide what he wishes to carve first, but carefully examines the piece of jade on hand and determines the most creative use he can make of it. According to the craftsman, one of the qualities of jade is that it "reveals itself." Small brown spots in the stone may become the eyes of an animal; varied brown veins, the bark of a tree.

Jade is an extremely hard stone and special abrasives and cutting tools are needed to carve it. The first primitive carving tools were probably bamboo drills with fine quartz sand used as an abrasive. Later, craftsmen added bronze tips to the bamboo. Eventually a special wire saw was devised which is still in use today for cutting crude blocks of jade. It is made from a single strand of wire held tightly between the ends of a curved piece of bamboo. The saw is pulled back and forth across the stone while keeping the cut lubricated with water and carborundum powder. If the jade is a pebble it must first be "skinned" to remove the dull, outer layer. This is done on a special jade workbench that has not changed in design over the centuries. The bench carries a horizontal shaft that revolves and to which the various cutting tools devised especially for cutting jade are attached.

Skinning is done with a steel wheel attached to the bench shaft. The operator holds the pebble in his right hand against the underside of the disk. In his left hand, he holds the wet carborundum mixture which he applies to the edge of the wheel. The preliminary operations of cutting and skinning jade are done by apprentices, though still under the watchful eye of the master craftsman. With this preliminary work done, the carving is completely in the hands of the master.

The main step of shaping is called *ya t'o*, and from this point on there is close cooperation between the designer and the carver. As the stone reveals itself, modifications in the design may well be needed. For the shaping, the craftsman uses a variety of cutting wheels varying in diameter from one half to three inches. The piece being carved is held in the left hand so that the wet carborundum abrasion can be applied with the forefinger of the right hand.

The carving of vases and hollow objects requires considerable

Jim Kwan, has been a jade carver all his life. He has spent two years working on this carving and when it is completed, he intends to retire from his work as a teacher at the Peking Arts and Crafts Center.

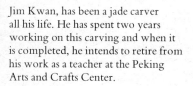

dexterity. The drill used is a piece of steel tubing attached to the bench shaft and filled with wet abrasive. The jade is held hard against the end of the revolving tube until the right depth has been reached. The core that has been drilled out is removed with a hammer and chisel. This is the most difficult part of all, for if the jade core is not struck at its edge with a sharp blow, pieces of core will be left behind and further laborious drilling will be necessary.

For high relief work and for shaping small objects little drills called *chuang ting* are used. It is with these drills that the jade craftsman brings his work to perfection. With them, a movable ring handle on a dish can be carved from a solid piece of jade – though only after weeks of patient attention. In the same way linked chains are fashioned from a piece of solid jade.

After several months of work, or years if the design is particularly intricate, the piece is ready for polishing. The first wheel or buffer, is called *chiao t'o* and is similar to a large grinding wheel, but made from a mixture of an adhesive such as shellac and a fine grade of carborundum. Buffers for the final polishing are made of different types and grades of leather. They come in all shapes and sizes so that even the most inaccessible parts of a carving can be reached.

The jade markets of Canton and Peking at the turn of the century, were a vivid illustration of the variety of carvings that were to be found in China. The Jade Market outside the Hatamen Gate in Peking attracted foreigners and craftsmen alike. Earrings, pendants, thumb rings and belt buckles were found in profusion. Little chains to be exchanged as tokens of friendship, and the curious "musical" jades could be bought there. The musical jades were pendants made of graded sizes of jade hung side by side. They were worn around the neck or hung from a belt and made a tinkling sound as the wearer

Left: Detail of a jade screen at the Kwangchow Trade Fair. Above: Carving a jade chain. Below: A finished jade bottle.

This chubby, cheerful Taoist monk is carved from soapstone.

walked along. Numerous open stalls lined the dusty, bustling streets of the market, yet amazingly nothing was ever stolen, for it was regarded as a public scandal if a merchant should lose a piece of jade through theft.

Some of the most popular items were jade carvings of the favorite symbolic objects of the Chinese people. The Peony, the Flower of Riches and Honor and an emblem of love and affection and the Pomegranate, symbolizing the hope of the family for numerous off-spring who will be both virtuous and famous were both popular. The deer and the tortoise were frequent themes used by the carver either sculpted as little statues or carved in relief.

There are, in fact, few of the popular symbols of folklore that cannot be found carved in jade and new themes have been added since the Revolution. The Chinese Government has set up jade studios in the old traditional centers, for it was felt that the craft had declined in the years since the last dynasty. As a result, the old traditional carvers are again brought together to pass on their skills to new apprentices. Once trained, they are encouraged to develop their own specialization in the craft carving modern designs that have been extended to portray the work and play of modern China as well as the traditional motifs of old China.

Like the jade market center in old Peking, the sector of Shanghai called Nantao or the Native City was a center of the ivory industry. If there was a profusion of different sorts of items carved in jade, then the list of things carved in ivory must be endless. The storefronts of the market were filled with every conceivable kind of ivoryware. The workshops were found at the rear of the store where

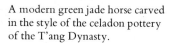

A modern green jade horse carved in the style of the celadon pottery of the T'ang Dynasty.

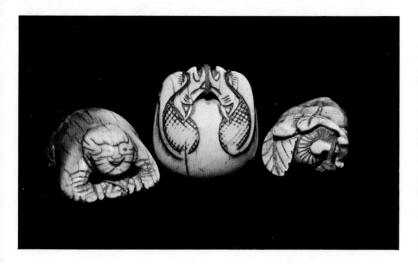

the members of a family would sit carving at a bench or sit on the ground patiently cutting pieces of elephant or walrus tusk into chopsticks, combs and mah-jong pieces. These did not require elaborate carving and supplied most of the craftsman's income. But in the store itself, half-hidden among the many carvings, the storekeeper would invariably have a bench at which he slowly worked on more delicate carvings for special customers. Elsewhere in the Native City, as in the other ivory centers of Foochow, Canton and Peking, were a few establishments producing decorative carvings that were far more intricate and delicately made. Whole families, often with hired help, devoted their lives to carving fine, exquisite figures of deities, mythical figures and folk heroes.

Ivory has been highly valued by the Chinese for centuries, though it does not possess the magical importance of jade. Ivory has been considered an indication of a man's wealth and status. In the first century A.D. it was used in payment of taxes and tribute to the

Left: Seventeenth century Chinese ivory netsuke. Above: Delicately tinted carved ivory. Below: A Fo dog holding a ball and surrounded by its pups.

Left: Young ivory carvers in Shanghai learn their trade beneath the watchful eye of the master.

Emperor. Only the aristocracy owned ivory in any quantity. A man of letters writing about this time tells how much status was attached to owning ivory. "The courtesans dip their slender fingers in ivory boxes containing perfumed cosmetics; the gourmets carry with them their own little ivory sticks for eating rice and the new rich hang their hats on ivory hatstands. Men of the world admire their favorite crickets through the delicate fretwork of ivory forming the lids of the special boxes carved out of gourds. I myself have bought a tiny bridge of ivory on which I rest my wrist while writing."

There could be, it seems, few uses to which the Chinese have not tried to put ivory. Medical etiquette in China once held it highly improper for a doctor to see the naked body of his female patients. Not only that, but it was considered indelicate for a lady to mention any part of her body to a doctor. A curious solution was developed. The doctor would carry with him specially carved ivory figures which revealed in intimate detail every part of the body. He would take these to the bedside of his patient, who put her hand through the curtain that hid her from the doctor and touched the part on the ivory statue that was causing her trouble.

Most of the ivory used in China today is imported, though elephants were once found there. Leading merchants financed long journeys to Burma, India and even as far as Africa to bring back ivory. African ivory was considered far superior to that from other places. It was important for the merchant to know how the elephant died, for this affected the quality of the material. If an elephant had been killed recently, then its ivory was considered superior. If, however, the animal had died naturally, it was important to know how long it had been dead to determine the grade of the ivory. Walrus ivory has been used since the time of the T'ang Dynasty, when it was given to the Emperor as tribute by the Tungus tribes of Manchuria. Chopsticks are frequently made from walrus tusk. Walrus ivory

The ivory carvers of Kwangchow are famed for their intricate filigree carving on whole elephant tusks.

Below right: Electric drills are now used to speed the production of fine carvings like this exquisite ivory boat.

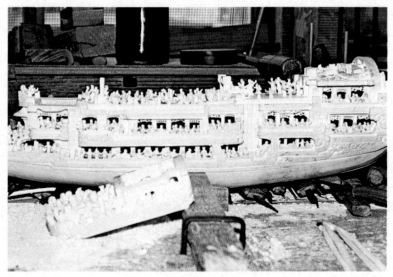

turns yellow with age and it was a simple matter to stain a carving with tea or tobacco juice to convince a buyer that the carved piece was very old.

The ivory carvers of Canton were once famed for their use of huge sections of elephant tusk. These were hollowed to an amazing thinness and the surface was carved with dainty filigree. A three-foot length of tusk was often carved into a series of elephants diminishing in size down the length of the tusk. "Spheres within spheres" or *tao-ch'in* is one of the more ingenious ivory carvings that originated in Canton and is still produced today. Tao-ch'in is a series of detached spheres one within the other and each with its surface carved in an intricate openwork design. The work is begun by carving a solid ball out of ivory. The ball is then pierced from several directions toward the center. Little knives are thrust in through the holes and a central sphere, about half an inch in diameter, is cut away from the solid mass until it is free to revolve inside. Using fine pointed tools, delicate patterns are then cut into the surface of this inner ball. The process is repeated until there are as many as 24 exquisitely carved inner spheres. The smallest ball in the center is solid but the hollow spheres are carved with delicate filigree patterns.

Peking ivory carvers, still renowned today, were once devoted to producing ivory that was said to approach a high level of art. The tradition dates back to the early Ch'ing Dynasty, when the Emperor Kang Hsi established a special workshop to supply his court with ivory. These craftsmen, brought in from all over China, were able to give their skill and imagination free rein. Each piece was highly ornamented in relief with figures of birds, animals, flowers, fruit and even Chinese characters which formed poems. Peking ivory is sometimes delicately colored with dyes and pigments using an elaborate technique called *lou-k'ung* which originated in this city. The ivory can be carved so that the design appears recessed in a shell or concavity.

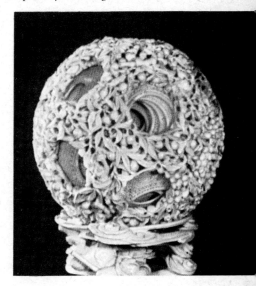

The tools of the ivory carver are similar to those used by the jade carver, though special abrasives are not needed because ivory is quite soft. The particular skill of ivory carving lies in the ability to use the

Right: Simple but efficient drills of ancient design are still used.

A skilled ivory carver uses a large number of tools each with a differently shaped blade.

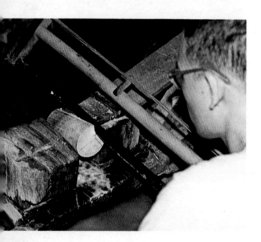

Large chunks of rough ivory are first sawn into smaller pieces.

Nowadays, women as well as men have the chance to learn ancient skills and become masters of ivory carving.

grain of the ivory as an intimate part of the design. Toward the end of the dynasties, so much ivory carving was being produced for export, that little attention was paid to using the texture and grain, and the resulting work was white and lifeless. The recent revival of ivory crafting, though still mainly for export, has brought back with it some of these traditional skills. Today, skilled craftsmen work in craft centers in many parts of China continuing to produce the breathtakingly beautiful carvings for which China is renowned.

The Chinese, ever with an eye to improving on nature in their arts and crafts, have always been eager to explore the possibilities of working with other, less common materials. Tortoiseshell, called *fai-mei*, has been used in fortune-telling since ancient times. When the shell was heated and then allowed to cool, cracks would develop from which the future could be divined.

The craft of working the shell depends on its property of softening when placed in hot water or when it is gently heated. The shell can then be stretched, bent, molded, split apart and welded together.

The shell used in China today is imported from the Indian Ocean and comes in little plates of separated shell. The tools of the craftsman are quite simple. In Kwangchow, where the craft is mainly practiced, these are a file, a chisel and a small saw. Most important of all are a pair of iron pliers with broad, smooth blades. The craftsman heats the pliers and uses them to weld the plates of shell together. Tortoiseshell is fashioned into incredibly intricate decorative carvings which are exported all over the world.

Stone carving, using a stone found in Chingtien County in the province of Chekiang, has recently been revived. The skill needed to carve the stone is not too different from that needed to carve jade, for the stone comes in a wide variety of colors, textures and grain. The stone is carved in two principal ways, two-dimensional relief carvings and three-dimensional, free-standing shapes. Tiny sculptures of human figures, flowers and stylized landscapes are frequently carved, as well as articles of daily use such as ashtrays, brush holders and small vases. Four new stone carving studios have been established recently in Chingtien providing work for some three hundred full-time artists.

The wood of the peach stone is one of the favorite woods for carving in China. The peach is an ancient symbol of immortality and springtime and is an emblem of marriage. The most felicitious time for marriage was considered to be the spring when the first peach trees blossom. The peach stones are intricately carved into little beads which were once worn by children to protect them from death.

Three thousand years of skilled tradition in carving the natural materials available to the craftsman has not been lost. Through the patient efforts of the old craftsmen teaching the new and the eagerness of the young craftsmen the craft has not only revived but often surpasses the technical skill and imagination of the old masters. New themes and old now combine to ensure that the Chinese craft of carving will continue to provide the world with works of unsurpassed beauty.

Cranes, a symbol of longevity, are here carved from soapstone.

Left: Carved peachstone beads were once worn by children to ward off death. Below: A tiny boat, carved from a peachstone.

CHAPTER 3

LAND
OF THE
SILK PEOPLE

"The Seres make precious, figured garments, resembling in color the flowers of the field, and rivaling the work of spiders," wrote Dionysius Peregetes, a Greek monk who lived 1900 years ago. Serinda, Sereca and Land of the Seres, describe one land and its people; China, land of the Silk People. These were the names used by the Greeks and Romans when they spoke of the Chinese. Certainly there was no cloth known to the Western world that could rival silk from China, and it became a highly prized possession.

The Chinese kept their secret for some 500 years after they began trading with the West. Then during the sixth century, it is said that some Indian monks who had lived in China smuggled out the eggs of the silkworm in a hollow tube and took them to the Byzantine Empire. Had they been caught, the penalty would have been death. Yet the secrets of silk have been known by the Chinese for more than 4000 years. Chinese folklore tells that it was the legendary Empress Hsi Ling Shih, wife of the Yellow Emperor, who, about the middle of the third millennium B.C., is supposed to have taught the people how to treat the cocoons and the silk to make clothes for themselves.

White silk is spun from the cocoons of the silk caterpillar and it seems likely that the first silk was made using broken threads from empty cocoons, which had been damaged by the escaping silkmoth. Even the early silkworm farmers may have allowed the moth to escape until by some happy accident someone discovered that the unbroken cocoons were one, long strand of silk. The silkworm is a temperamental creature and will spin its best quality silk only under the most favorable conditions. As a result, the process of sericulture, the production of raw silk from silkworms, is a very delicate one, and throughout China's history it has always been performed by women.

The phoenix encircles the peony with its tail in this modern Chinese embroidery.

Opposite: An artist in a Peking appliqué and embroidery workshop prepares a new design.

Above: Silkworms feed on fresh mulberry leaves. Right: Silk cocoons are inspected and sorted.

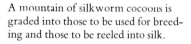

A mountain of silkworm cocoons is graded into those to be used for breeding and those to be reeled into silk.

When the silkmoth lays its eggs, they are collected and kept cold to prevent them from hatching before the end of April. Ten days of incubation are needed before the eggs hatch into minuscule worms only as thick as a human hair. These are brushed into bamboo baskets where they are fed a diet solely of fresh mulberry leaves. Two kinds of mulberry tree are cultivated to ensure the highest quality and quantity of leaves. *Yeh sang*, the wild mulberry, is a hardy tree producing few leaves, while *lu sang*, the domestic mulberry, yields a lot of leaf but is a less hardy tree. Silkworms fed on yeh sang spin a coarse, inferior silk. The Chinese therefore sow fruits of the wild mulberry and later graft the domestic variety onto the saplings. The result is a hardy tree producing numerous high quality leaves. It has been estimated that it takes one ton of leaves to feed one ounce of newly hatched worms, which in turn spin about 130 pounds of cocoons yielding 12 pounds of silk.

For 35 days the silkworms do nothing but eat. During this time they molt four times. At the end of this time when they are about two inches long, they are placed on inclined straw trays, where

It is a tradition that only women work with silk cocoons.

Gleaming skeins of silk prepared at Shia Chiao commune are now ready for dyeing and weaving. Most of the commune's silk is exported.

they begin spinning their cocoons. After five days the cocoons are ready and the best are selected for breeding purposes. The moth hatches after ten days, mates, lays its eggs and dies all in one day. Only about half of the remaining cocoons are fine enough to produce reeled silk and the rest are used to make what is called "refuse" silk, an inferior quality of silk. The process of reeling now begins. The cocoons are placed in hot water, which partly dissolves the sericin, a gelatinous substance that the silkworm produces to bind the filaments of its cocoon together. The water is stirred with a bamboo comb, which catches the ends of the filaments, and the cocoons begin to unravel as the comb is lifted from the water. The number of filaments separated varies according to the quality of silk to be reeled.

Cocoons which do not unwind into an unbroken thread of silk are used as refuse or inferior grade silk. Here, these expanded cocoons are hung out to dry.

The most delicate silk uses six to eight, whereas a coarser product requires 25 to 30.

Gently, with short tugs, several yards of filament are unwound and taken up by hand. The first few layers of the cocoon to be unraveled are called surface floss. These are broken off to produce refuse silk after spinning. When the operator is satisfied that the surface floss has been removed she leads the filaments to a treadle-operated reeling machine, through an eye, to form a single thread. The silk is wound into skeins and is ready for dyeing, weaving and marketing.

The actual stitches used in Chinese embroidery are not different from those used in the West but it is through their skill in using these stitches and in their choice of colors that the Chinese have created a highly original form of embroidery. The earliest used stitch was chain stitch and its two variations. One is an open chain stitch with very broad loops and the other a combination of chain stitch and split stitch giving a double-chain effect. These date back to the Han Dynasty.

Satin stitch, which came to be used later, was called *t'ao chen*, or enveloping stitch, for long floats of untwisted floss silk were used extending some distance across the fabric to show the stitch to the best advantage. The best Chinese satin stitch is perfect, both in its shading and spidery fineness. The satin stitch creates double-sided embroidery, embroidery which is the same on both sides. It is considered wasteful for many purposes, so that frequently a surface satin stitch is used. Long and short satin stitches are used by Chinese embroiderers with astounding success. Occasionally the satin stitch is raised by working it over a foundation of coarser thread or over a padding of cloth or paper. This padded satin stitch is often used

The Chinese lady in this nineteenth century print works on her embroidery.

Below: Bobbins of colored silk hang above this young embroiderer's head.

Below right: Designers at work in a Peking handicraft factory that produces various needlework.

to accentuate details such as animals' eyes and flower centers.

Couching was first used over a thousand years ago in the T'ang Dynasty. Gold and silver wire had not been developed at that time, so gold or silver foil was pasted onto paper or fine animal skin and cut into small strips. These were laid on the surface of the fabric and sewn down with small stitches of fine silk. So that this stitching could be as unobtrusive as possible, red silk thread was used for gold foil and white thread for silver foil. Later, the metal foil was wound around a core of red silk thread, and occasionally yellow thread was used for the stitching. Couching is traditionally used for outlining floral and animal designs, in spirals representing the sun and the center of flowers, and in solid embroidered sections for particularly rich cloud or sea effects.

The Peking knot, often mistaken in the West for a French knot, has two uses for the Chinese embroiderer. These small spots of color are used to intensify hues, particularly when not set too close together. The Peking knot is also used to pick out details in areas of satin stitch, providing a rough contrast to the smooth surface of the rest of the embroidery. The Peking knot is made with a fairly heavy thread and uses only a single turn around the needle, making a small ring rather than a seedlike knot. Other traditional stitches used are flame or Florentine stitch, called *ch'o sha*, tent stitch, outline or stem stitch and counted canvas stitch, which in China is done on gauze rather than canvas.

The Chinese take particular delight in bright colors and to Western eyes the combinations of colors may seem garish at first. However, color, like form, has meaning to the Chinese. The choice of color is not based on a color wheel but on the intimate association of colors and their symbolic significance and relationships. Red and yellow,

Left: An outline is drawn up from the original painted design.

Above: Skilled embroiderers stitch fine strands of silk into a mass of shimmering flowers.

Below: The Buddhist emblems of the Wheel of Law and the Umbrella are part of this Ch'ing Dynasty gold couching embroidery.

Flowers and a butterfly are embroidered in the vibrant colors beloved by the Chinese.

Above: Using traditional methods, the modern embroiderer achieves a realism not found in the work of ancient China.

Symbol of purity, the lotus rises above the dark of the muddiest waters.

for instance, would seem reasonable choices for the color of the sun and moon, yet the Chinese would say that in using these colors they are not simply copying nature. Instead, they would say that the sun is inhabited by the phoenix, whose natural color is red, and the moon is inhabited by the hare, which is the incarnation of an Imperial consort whose natural color is yellow.

The points of the compass, north, south, east and west are represented by the colors black, red, blue and white. Water, fire and earth are given the colors green, red and white. The combinations are numerous but the associations of color and symbol are fixed by tradition and are not varied despite the perhaps overly bright contrasts. It has been said though, that the Chinese had an eye to the future when they used bright colors, for in time the colors fade somewhat and this mellowing of color frequently adds a final perfect touch to an embroidery.

Chinese embroiderers have called almost entirely on natural forms for their design inspiration. They have, however, never slavishly copied nature, for it is believed that perfect art improves on nature. As their designs evolved over the centuries, these would be remembered and passed on to the next generation. From about the fourteenth century these patterns were recorded in books specially for the use of embroiderers. The favorite flowers of embroiderers are the peach, pomegranate, narcissus and lotus. The lotus, regarded as sacred both in its use and its beauty, is an emblem of summer and fruitfulness and in some embroideries may be so stylized as to look like a peony.

Birds, bats and butterflies frequently appear in embroidery patterns. The bat has a special place in Chinese motifs, for unlike countries where bats are associated with evil, in China this animal is an emblem of happiness. When four bats are depicted together they represent the Four Joys:

The peacock, kingfisher and duck, some of the birds in this modern embroidery are favorites with the Chinese because of the brilliance of their plumage.

A group of five bats are the Five Happinesses or Blessings of old age, wealth, health, love of virtue and a natural death. The butterfly is traditionally an emblem of joy.

Cranes and pine trees are embroidered together as symbols of longevity and old age and a pair of mandarin ducks indicate a happy marriage. The peacock symbolizes beauty and dignity and the Decoration of the Peacock Feather was given by the Emperor at one time for services to society. The beautiful daughter of Tou I, a military commander in 562 A.D., is said to have painted a peacock on a screen and offered to marry any man who could hit the bird twice in succession. The Emperor shot both eyes with his first two arrows and in China the phrase "choosing by hitting the bird screen" came to mean choosing a husband.

The Dragon is perhaps the best known motif in Chinese design. It is also the most important, for unlike the dragon of the West, which is a creature of evil and destruction, the Chinese dragon represents the forces of nature and is the essence of strength and beauty. He lives,

A Mandarin square for the robe of a civil official of the Ch'ing Dynasty.

Subtle colors together with consummate skill produce a superb piece of embroidery.

A dragon chasing a flaming pearl was one of the most important of the ancient Chinese symbols and often featured in embroidery.

according to mythology, hidden deep inside mountains, or coiled in the deepest oceans awaiting the time when he must awaken. His claws can be seen in the fork of lightning bolts and his scales in the bark of rain-swept trees. His voice can be heard in the hurricane that scatters the dead leaves of winter so hurrying on the spring.

There are three kinds of dragon, the *lung*, which inhabits the sky, the *li*, which lives in the ocean, and *chiao*, a scaly dragon found in marshy places. The lung is the most powerful of all and its breath has the appearance of a cloud which can turn to water or fire. Its voice is said to be like the jingling of copper pans. This dragon is believed to ride upon the clouds and is frequently portrayed chasing a pearl or round fiery object, which was believed to be the sun. If he loses the pearl the dragon loses his power. Eclipses of the sun were thought to occur when the dragon swallowed the pearl.

Like the dragon, the phoenix, sometimes called the "Bird of Gorgeous Plumage," is one of the supernatural creatures. The Chinese believed that the phoenix lived in the Vermilion Hills, eating and drinking, waiting for peace in the country, for it appears in times of peace and prosperity. Because the phoenix presides over the South it symbolizes sun and warmth for the summer and the harvest. The phoenix is said to have appeared at the time Confucius was born.

The dragon was also the personal emblem of Emperors and the phoenix the motif of Empresses and were always embroidered or woven into their robes. Some form of dragon was, in fact, always embroidered on the robes of Imperial Court officials. Since the reign of Kao Tsu in the Han Dynasty, the five-clawed dragon was used by the Emperor, his sons and princes of the first and second rank.

Princes of the third and fourth rank used the four-clawed *mang* dragon while lesser officials were only allowed to represent themselves by a serpentlike creature with five claws. These specific emblems of rank eventually faded and the royal court was symbolized by a five-clawed dragon, since it was unthinkable to use the inferior mang dragon.

From Ming times onward, court robes became masterpieces of embroidery and not without reason. The robe itself was a complete sum of symbols – the symbolism of the quality of the textile, in the form, color and pattern of the robe. The symbolic meaning of the robe is explained in a Chinese book on etiquette. "The roundness of the sleeves reminded the wearer that when he raised his hands while walking, his manners should be elegant. The straightness of the seam at the back and the rectangles of the embroidered collar reminded the wearer that his administration should be impeccable and his justice incorruptible. The lower edge of the robe which was horizontal like the beam of a balance, signified that the will was to be firm and the heart always calm."

Every court official was entitled to wear either a dragon robe or a court robe depending on the occasion. The dragon robe was a semi-formal gown for dinners and receptions, and the court robe was for

Left: Sacred symbols adorn this nineteenth century Emperor's robe.

ceremonial occasions such as the Emperor's birthday. Both carried the dragon as the principal motif. The rank of a court official was indicated by the use of particular motifs, other than the dragon. These were embroidered on so-called "mandarin squares" which could be attached to the back and front of a robe. Nobles and military officers took animals as their motifs, while civil officials used birds. The crane, *hsien-ho*, was worn by civil officials of the fourth grade, and was embroidered as a white bird with a black head tinged with scarlet. Sometimes it is seen carrying the peach of immortality in its beak. Civil officials of the fifth grade wore a silver pheasant, *pai-hsien*, a white bird with dark blue or green crest and between two and five long, slender tail plumes.

Whatever the creatures represented, they are embroidered in a natural setting with rocks or earth and waves symbolizing the sea. A cloud-filled sky completes the meaning of the whole – the Universe in microcosm. Mandarin squares were embroidered on a rectangular frame supported on two uprights and were usually stitched by men and boys for they had stronger fingers. Court officials would have them made to order from private workshops, whereas Imperial insignia were made in the Imperial Silk Factories. The squares could be detached from the robe, which was particularly useful in the spring when silk robes were replaced by lighter, gauze robes. Mandarin squares were also made in two halves so that they could lie across the open front of some court robes.

An Emperor's Summer Robe was one of the most beautiful of all court garments. Made from bright yellow silk, it was embroidered

Above: An eighteenth century print shows a Chinese lady of the time busy quilting stockings.

Below: An embroidered golden pheasant embellishes this pair of Mandarin squares.

The eight sacred Buddhist emblems.

with the Twelve Imperial Symbols of sun, moon, constellations, mountain, the *fu* symbol, the ax, flowery bird, paired dragons, water weed, temple cups, millet and flames as well as the dragon. These symbolized the supreme powers and qualities of the Emperor. The sun and moon were placed on either side of the collar with the constellations above the dragon's head. The fu motif, a symbol of peaceful collaboration, was embroidered near the dragon's tail, and the ax, a symbol of justice, was placed just opposite.

The Four Bats could be found among the clouds, while the deep sea was represented by brightly colored vertical stripes. The Earth is shown as highly stylized mountains rising from the sea. Many other traditional motifs are found scattered across the robe, including the Eight Taoist Immortals and the Eight Buddhist Emblems. The latter are made up of the Wheel of Law, the Conch shell, Umbrella, Lotus flower, Vase, Canopy, a Pair of Fishes and the Mystic Knot. A symbol of longevity, the Mystic Knot is said also to represent the sacred intestines of the Buddha.

The Imperial weaving factories were once at Hangchow and Soochow. The looms on which the robes were made were much larger

Embroidery motifs today reflect a new China with different motifs and symbols, though the skill of the embroiderer is just as impressive.

than the ordinary loom and in addition employed a large super-structure called *hua-lou* or pattern tower, some fifteen feet high. Two trained men sat in this superstructure and raised the successive sets of loom harness to make the pattern. Considerable exactness was required for this task.

The techniques of embroidery used in modern China have changed little. Traditional stitches are still used to create delicate and exquisitely detailed embroidery. The four modern centers of embroidery are in Soochow and the provinces of Hunan, Kwangtung and Szechwan. Soochow is famed for its double-sided embroidery worked on fine, transparent, nylon fabric. This intricate stitching requires finer silk thread than ordinary embroidery, and the skilled craftsman splits each thread into up to forty-eight almost invisible, separate strands. Completing a piece of double-sided embroidery takes months of work. Both sides of the work are identical and perfect so that the embroidery can be displayed in a glass frame. The subjects for which Soochow embroidery is best known are fluffy white cats with one blue and one brown eye and delicate goldfish floating in fronds of seaweed.

Themes from modern China are now frequent subjects for the embroiderer, who adapts the traditional stitches to contemporary scenes to achieve a realism not found in the embroidery of old China. The best known motifs in embroideries of this kind include "The Chengtu-Kunming Railway" and "The Yangtze Bridge." Linen or cotton handkerchiefs are embroidered in Swatow mainly for export, though these elegant handkerchiefs are also popular at home.

The chief use of embroidery in China today is for screens and wall decorations in public buildings. Always searching for new effects, the modern Chinese embroiderers have adapted and evolved this ancient craft to a level of perfection and beauty previously unknown.

Chen Tsai-Hsien of the Soochow Embroidery Institute works on a delicate embroidery which will take months to complete. Soochow is famed for its double-sided embroidery worked with silk thread so fine that it is almost invisible. Fluffy kittens and delicate goldfish are typical of the subjects that are worked in this way.

MAKING THE CRAFTS OF CHINA

Throughout this book you will find "how-to" sections that give step by step instructions for making some of the Chinese crafts you have been reading about. These crafts projects are replicas of authentic Chinese folk crafts and are true to the traditional colors and patterns of the country. The materials and techniques suggested are as similar as possible to those used by native craftsmen. If materials and tools are difficult to find, we have recommended easily available substitutes that will be found around the house or that can be bought at hardware and hobby stores. Photographs and detailed diagrams show exactly how to make each crafts project. And each how-to section includes a selection of other traditional patterns and motifs so that you can adapt and vary the projects to create ethnic crafts that are both authentic and personal.

Enlarging and reducing designs

Make a drawing or tracing of the original design. Enclose the design in a box. Divide the box horizontally and vertically into quarters. Divide the quarters again, and again if necessary, until the whole design is covered with a grid of small squares. Draw another box to the size of the finished design. Divide the second box into a grid with exactly the same number of squares as the original grid.

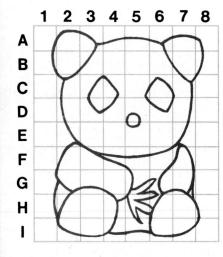

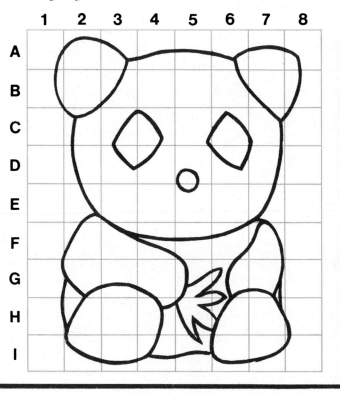

Copy outlines of the design from the first grid to the second. Mark numbers and letters along the side of the grids to keep track of the design and make it easier to identify each square.

IMPERIAL DRAGON MOTIF

To embroider the Imperial Dragon, you will need three types of gold thread, the thickest to outline the dragon, a medium-fine, twisted thread to fill in solid areas and a medium-fine smooth thread for the scales. Use red and pale yellow fine silk thread for the couching. Draw the silk across a lump of beeswax before sewing to protect it against snags from the metal thread. Use a fine embroidery needle for couching and a large-eyed needle to pull the gold thread to the underside of the fabric. Outline the design on the fabric using basting stitches or dressmakers' carbon paper and a tracing wheel, depending on the type of fabric you are working with.

Couching is an effective and elegant embroidery method for Chinese motifs. This work is done on fine silk, although heavier fabrics such as brocade, damask, satin and velvet also make ideal background materials.

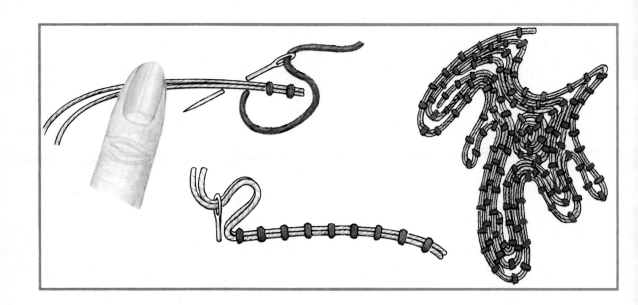

To begin couching, lay the gold thread along the line of the design. When couching fine gold thread, use two threads together; the effect is the same and the work progresses faster. Secure the couching thread on the underside, bring it to the right side and take a small stitch over the gold thread. Keep the couching stitches small and evenly spaced. After completing the couching, pierce the fabric with a stiletto or large needle and take both ends of the gold thread through to the underside of the fabric. To fill a solid area with couching, work the outline first and then spiral inward, curving and folding the gold thread closely and neatly as you sew.

Couching must be worked with the fabric stretched tight in a frame. A large rectangular frame, like the one shown here, big enough to take the complete design is the best type to use. It can be supported on the knees and propped against a table leaving both hands free for the embroidery.

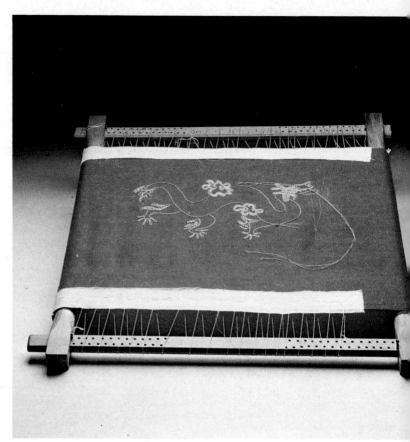

A selection of traditional designs of bats, butterflies and flowers make ideal subjects for embroidery. The designs can be enlarged following the instructions on page 42. Each design can be worked entirely in gold couching or in a combination of couching and other stitches such as satin stitch and stem stitch. If you have not attempted couching with gold thread before, any one of these designs could be simply outlined in gold and the details filled in with richly colored silk floss.

CHAPTER 4
THE SECRETS
OF THE
POTTER

Climbing the foothills around modern Shekwan in Kwangtung Province can be seen the famous, but now derelict "dragon kilns," which once produced some of China's most beautiful ceramics. Similar kilns are found around the town of Tingshan, and until quite recently two of them were still being operated, though there are plans to close them down and replace them with more modern kilns.

For centuries ceramics have been one of China's most prolific craft industries and though there was a decline in the quality of the wares produced in the early decades of this century, many of the traditional centers of the craft have now been revived. The most famous of these centers is Ching-te Chen in Kiangsi Province, which even in the seventeenth century was a great ceramic metropolis. The fame and splendor of Chinese ceramics has been the result of both luck and skill – luck in having among her natural resources some of the finest clays in the world and skill in utilizing these unique resources in a way that remains unsurpassed today.

The making of pottery vessels and figures is always one of the first crafts to flourish in a culture, and China therefore developed this craft very early in history. The most primitive pottery was made by building up circular vessels from ropes or coils of clay which were then smoothed into each other to make the surface even. When a device was invented for rotating the pot while it was being made, probably a pivoted table or wooden disk that could be slowly turned by an assistant, it allowed the potter to make more uniform pottery. This fairly primitive device eventually developed into a true potter's wheel and pottery became a highly skilled craft: an act of communication between the potter's hands and the rapidly spinning mass of clay before him. The Chinese potter has been unique, for although devices have been used in other countries for judging the symmetry and trueness of a particular pottery form, these were never used in

Today's craftsmen are encouraged to maintain and improve upon the traditional techniques when making wares such as this porcelain vase.

Opposite: A pottery factory in Fushan, near Kwangchow, which has been a ceramics center for hundreds of years.

49

One of a series of nineteenth century paintings of the ceramic process shows the potter working at his wheel.

This bowl of Kuang Tung ware dates from the late eighteenth century.

China. Shapes and designs were judged entirely by eye as they formed on the wheel and in this way the Chinese potter has created a wealth of elaborate, intricate and daring forms.

Many shapes cannot be produced on the potter's wheel. Human and animal figures and complicated floral arrangements must either be fashioned entirely by hand or by the use of intricate molds. The making of such molds is almost a craft in itself.

The presence of feldspar in some of the clays found in China led to the discovery of the uniquely Chinese ceramic, porcelain. Two naturally occurring minerals are used in the manufacture of procelain. The first is a white clay called kaolin, named after a hilly district near Ching-te Chen, where it is found in large quantities. *Pai-tun-tzu* or petuntse is a hard rock composed of quartz and feldspar and is the second essential ingredient for making porcelain. For centuries after the Chinese discovery of porcelain it was the lack of feldspar in the final mix that eluded European attempts to duplicate this treasured ceramic of the East. The name pai-tun-tzu means "little white blocks," for that is the shape into which the powdered rock was eventually formed for use by the potter. The Chinese call kaolin and petuntse "the bones and the flesh" of porcelain.

The making of a piece of finished, plain white porcelain from the crude clay mixture requires several stages. The first step is the preparation of the refined clay mixture. Ching-te Chen was fortunate in having deposits of high quality kaolin and petuntse close to its factories. Nevertheless, some refining of the clay was necessary and in earlier days this meant the pounding of a mixture of kaolin and water sometimes using water buffalo to supply the required energy. The clay and water mixture was placed in a large pit and the buffalo

encouraged to pound the mixture with their hooves. The animals would be stopped periodically, and a creamy, white layer of clay slip allowed to float to the surface. This was skimmed off and placed in another pit and the process repeated until no further clay rose to the surface. The finely divided clay particles were now ready to be mixed with the powdered petuntse. The final quality of the porcelain depends on the proportions in which the two ingredients are mixed. Fine quality porcelain requires equal proportions of the two, whereas medium quality product uses a mixture of six parts of petuntse to four parts of kaolin.

A blend of the two ingredients is placed into an enormous bowl, beaten with a large spatula and then kneaded. This is the most crucial part in the preparation of the clay, for the final product must be entirely free from bubbles and grains of sand. Such impurities in the clay could cause the porcelain to crack in the kiln.

The clay is then shaped using two methods, the wheel and the mold. Early processes were very much like a modern assembly line, for the first laborer would partly shape a cup on the wheel. A second craftsman finished the piece using a mold into which it was pressed. A third worker thinned and smoothed the clay, while a fourth might add on a pre-fabricated handle. Complex shapes might be handled by up to seventy workers.

The shaping of the clay was not necessarily complete at this stage. One of the most delicate types of porcelain, called eggshell or *t'o-t'ai*, meaning "without a body," can be finally formed only when the clay has dried to what potters call "leather hardness." At this point the craftsman will gradually pare and scrape the body of the vessel until the walls are so thin they are nearly transparent.

51

Firing the porcelain in brick-built kilns; the ceramic process is faithfully recorded in this series of prints.

Below and right: Scenes in a Fushan pottery, one of 14 in the area today. Ornaments, tiles, domestic utensils and objects are all made here from glazed stoneware. The traditional red-glazed pottery is baked in wood-fired kilns. Over half of the factory's produce is intended for export.

If the porcelain is to be simply a plain, undecorated white, it is now ready to be glazed. The discovery of glazes was probably entirely accidental. It is probable that the Chinese discovered glazing by noticing that some pots came out of the kiln with a glossy surface caused by a fall of wood ash onto the pot. Glaze is simply a hard transparent layer baked onto the surface of the vessel or figure and it is the skilled use of certain kinds of glaze that has made Chinese ceramics a particularly outstanding craft. Porcelain glaze is made from petuntse, which is washed with water, broken into small pieces and then pulverized in a mortar. To complete the glaze, limestone and vegetable matter such as bracken, was burned in heaps and the resulting lime and vegetable ash was mixed with water and powdered petuntse. Small objects were glazed by dipping them in this mixture while larger ones were either painted with glaze or sprayed with glaze through a bamboo tube.

What makes porcelain so different from other ceramics is the fact that both the body and the glaze contain feldspar and that when the two are fired together at a particular temperature they fuse, leaving no distinction between the body and the glaze. Porcelain must not

Left: Unglazed porcelain is painted in this nineteenth century print. Above: A young boy makes a series of porcelain miniatures. Below: The Dragon kilns of southern China.

only be fired at a particular temperature, about 1300°C, but also in a particular atmosphere. In any kiln two kinds of atmosphere are possible. One is an "oxidizing" atmosphere, in which air is freely admitted to the kiln and the other a "reducing" atmosphere, in which the supply of air is restricted by closing off the kiln at a critical point in the firing. It is this latter type that is necessary for porcelain.

Kilns used before the beginning of this century varied in design between northern China and southern China. In the North, kilns were constructed as single kilns grouped together, while those of the South were dragon kilns. Essentially these were a series of connected chambers, built on a hillside, each higher than the one before, with the number of chambers varying from between ten and twelve. The main fire box was located at the lowest end of the kiln and it was therefore the lower chambers that were fired first. Pottery from these chambers was usually inferior to that from the upper sections, for the higher chambers warmed up more gradually and evenly. Firing of the entire kiln could take up to twenty days, and it has been estimated that a dragon kiln could hold 25,000 pieces at a time.

Pottery, particularly porcelain, to be fired in these kilns was placed

A modern bowl of egg shell porcelain.

in strong earthenware molds, called saggars. These had to match the exact size of the article placed in them, and the modeling of these earthenware shapes was so difficult that only a few people in each pottery center were capable of making them well.

At one time, each kiln had its head keeper or *pa-chuang-t'ou*, who was also a pottery "baker." These bakers were divided into hot fire men, slow fire men and circulating fire men. An old Chinese pottery book tells us that the fire in the kiln must be "hot and strong" for the wares to cook evenly, it must be "small and slow" or the moisture in the clay will not dry by degrees, and unless the heat circulates freely, the clay cannot be thoroughly baked.

The methods used for the decoration of ceramics are very diverse and a single piece may use a combination of techniques. The simplest technique is the use of colored glazes. With porcelain the color choice is limited because of the high temperature at which the clay is baked. Oxides of iron, copper and cobalt are used for these high fired glazes and the color produced depends on the atmosphere of the kiln. In a reducing atmosphere, iron produces a beautiful pale green glaze that resembles jade to which the name "celadon ware" has been given, while under oxidizing conditions, yellow, russet-browns and black are obtained. Copper, in reducing conditions, produces a blood-red color, whereas cobalt creates a characteristic blue over a range of temperatures.

Though these represent a limited selection of colors available to the craftsman, the actual effects that could be obtained were many and varied. It must be remembered that unlike the modern color chemist, who can use pure chemicals to obtain pure colors, the Chinese potter, even until well into this century was using impure ores and minerals for his color effects. In fact it was the impurities in his materials that produced results characteristic only of Chinese wares. Even imperfections in his technique, which he learned to reproduce, can give certain effects that are found in no other ceramic in the world. For instance, the best celadon ware has thousands of minute bubbles in the glaze that could have been removed if the piece had been fired longer. Cobalt ore, ground by hand into grains of uneven size, gives softer, more subtle tones of blue than ore which has been ground to even grains by mechanical means. And certain glazes can show a crackle effect caused by a different rate of cooling between the body and the glaze. No doubt the effect was discovered entirely by accident, yet the Chinese potter has, out of this, created a whole new technique in which he is able to vary the extent and the size of the crackle on the surface.

For painted decoration the potter had two basic techniques at his disposal – underglaze and overglaze painting. "Blue and white" porcelain is perhaps one of the best known examples of underglaze painting and it is a style that potters in many countries have tried to copy. Quite simply, the blue pigment from cobalt ore is applied to the unglazed, unfired clay piece, which is then allowed to dry

A Kuan vase with crackled glaze from the Sung Dynasty.

A plate from a nineteenth century trades album shows a jar being painted.

before being covered with a clear glaze. When the clay is fired and fusion of the glaze and body is complete, the blue design seems suspended between the outer surface and the body. Painting onto unfired clay is an extremely skillful task, for the clay absorbs the paint immediately and the artist must be both deft and bold in his strokes.

Overglaze painting requires a second firing, for the piece is first glazed and fired and then painted with enamel colors that require a lower temperature firing than underglaze colors to fuse the color into the glaze. The favorite enamel colors used are cobalt-blue, copper-green, iron-red, manganese-purple and pinks or crimson produced from gold.

Painting is not the only decorative technique of the potter. The unfired clay could be carved or have designs impressed upon the surface. A particularly delicate technique requires rice grains to be

Left: Details are hand painted onto the porcelain. The blue and white plate and vase are typical of the modern porcelain that China produces for export to other countries.

Water power is harnessed to pound and refine the raw kaolin used to make fine Chinese porcelain.

55

Such is the Chinese craftsman's love of ornament that even this public trash barrel is finely embellished.

pressed through the surface of the clay leaving small holes. The piece is then glazed so that each hole is filled with glaze and fired leaving a lattice-work of tiny transparent windows. Another technique used was to place a leaf inside a bowl to be fired. The leaf acted as a fluxing agent which caused the glaze underneath to melt more easily and left a ghostly outline on the glaze.

The motifs used for the decoration of ceramics are almost endless and cover the entire spectrum of Chinese traditional symbols. Flower decorations are particularly appealing. A popular tree is the plum, which blossoms at about the time of the Chinese New Year and the bamboo, which lends itself well to the kind of brush strokes used in forming Chinese characters. Groups of objects painted on vessels

A vase from the K'ang-hsi Dynasty with an underglaze decoration in red and blue.

Perfect copies of ancient ceramic masterpieces are now being produced such as these sleek, lifelike tigers which receive their finishing touches from a skilled artisan.

Women put the finishing touches to contemporary tricolor horses and figures modeled on the masterpieces of ancient ceramic art of the T'ang Dynasty.

A pot of flowers at the Ming Tombs, burial place of the old emperors.

may have hidden meanings – the magnolia, quince and tree peony painted together are read as "May you dwell in Jade Halls and enjoy wealth and honors." Taoist myths and legends provide many of the figures and scenes depicted on pottery. The Taoist Eight Immortals are well known figures, often shown with the God of Longevity, Shou Lao, represented as an old man with a high forehead, holding a peach and a staff and often riding an ox. Many Taoist tales and plays are found portrayed around the sides of vases and bowls.

Each dynasty throughout Chinese history has had its own designs, its favorite glazes and colors. Every dynasty chose to preserve the particular treasures of its predecessor as well as developing its own style. The present revival of pottery craft in China is no exception, for the Chinese government realized that unless the old techniques were taught now, there would be few craftsmen left who would remember and who could pass them on to the new generation of potters.

Eggshell porcelain is now made in Peking and Ching-te Chen and underglaze blue is produced in Shekwan. Perfect copies of Sung celadon ware are made in China today as are replicas of vibrant earthenware T'ang horses with their flaring nostrils and figures of sleek, lifelike tigers. In some centers, hand painting is being supplemented with the use of stencils and the incised rice designs are today reproduced with tiny knives rather than grains of real rice, yet the final product is of the same high quality as that produced in China centuries ago.

CHAPTER 5
SKILLS OF THE PUPPET MASTER

This little boy in his gaily embroidered shirt, lives in Shanghai.

Opposite: The hobbyhorse has a universal and timeless appeal as shown in this sixteenth century scroll painting.

On the fourth day of every month, outside the east wall of the old city of Peking, the Flower Market was held. It was so called not only because the flowers of the season were on sale, but because the women of the market wore paper flowers in their hair. One could be certain though, that many people had not come to this busy, colorful market to buy its many wares, but to see one man – the puppeteer.

Everyone, not just the children, would be waiting for his arrival by the city wall, for that was where he set up his portable theater. The puppeteer carried this little theater or booth, everywhere. It was quite simply a wooden beam or yoke that rested on his shoulders and supported the stage above the level of his head. A length of cloth was draped from three sides of the base of the stage down to his feet, concealing him completely from the audience. The back of the stage was supported by leaning it against the city wall. The stage itself represented an open-fronted Chinese house. When the show was ready to begin, the puppeteer would sound two little gongs from within his theater.

The Chinese puppet theater has a time-honored tradition going back perhaps 3000 years. No one knows quite how it began, but there are, of course, many tales surrounding its origins. The writer Chen Yuan during the Sung Dynasty tells us that the first puppets were made and puppet theater was performed at the court of the Chou Emperor Mu-wang about 1100 B.C. Legend has it that the puppets were made by Yang Shih, who was so skilled at his craft that at one performance before the Emperor it was thought that the puppets were winking at Mu-wang's concubines and he promptly ordered the puppeteer to be executed. Yang Shih quickly slashed his puppets with a knife to show the Emperor that they were not alive. The Emperor reprieved him, but was only partly mollified and ordered that the ladies of the court never watch another show. From

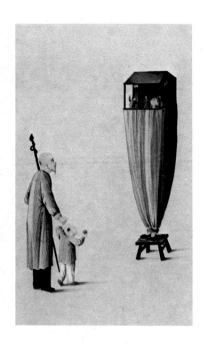

The traveling puppet master with his portable stage and skillfully manipulated finger puppets was a great attraction in old China.

that time onward it was a feudal custom never to allow women to watch a puppet show.

Another tale places the origins of puppetry at a later date, in the reign of the Emperor Kao-tzu in 262 B.C. At this time, the city of Pinchen, residence of the Emperor, was under siege by the Mongol warlord Khan Modo, and was in danger of being taken until one of the Emperor's courtiers came up with a crafty plan. Knowing that Khan Modo's wife was a jealous woman he ordered that a puppet be made in the shape of a beautiful maiden and by some ingenious contraption he caused the puppet to dance on the city walls. The Khan's wife, seeing this, believed the puppet to be alive and pestered her husband until he called off the siege, for she feared he might well take the maiden as his concubine when he captured the city.

The Chinese made four kinds of puppet: hand puppets, string-manipulated puppets, those worked by rods from below and shadow puppets. Chinese hand puppets are among the most perfectly proportioned, expressive and mobile puppets of any in the world. Unlike many Western puppets, they have much smaller heads, about two inches in diameter made of carved wood or molded clay. The heads are hollow to allow one finger to be placed inside them. Despite the small size they often have movable mouths and eyes, which requires considerable skill to operate with only one finger.

Some of the puppet characters have movable fingers. The hands are designed so that if the palm is turned upward, all the fingers are outstretched, whereas if the palm is turned downward, two or three fingers drop under their own weight. In a "male" puppet the hands are used with amazing effect to give an imperative gesture. In a

Characters from old legends come alive to re-enact their story under the puppet master's clever hands.

Hand puppets have moveable mouths and hands to lend greater realism to the play.

"female" puppet the same technique is used, but it is the index and little finger that are left outstretched to give a very ladylike pose.

The costumes of these hand puppets are highly elaborate and true to life even down to the intricate details of embroidery copied from traditional clothing. The puppets even had wigs of human hair arranged in accurate Chinese hairstyles.

The plays of the puppet theater abound with mythical stories, legends and love stories as well as song-and-dance routines. A favorite play for hand puppets is the story of Chu Pa-chieh and the

A selection of old Chinese puppets is displayed in an ornate wooden case.

The old, well-loved puppet tales are enacted in Chinese communities the world over, like this show in Penang, Malaysia.

Proud parents photograph their daughter beside the flowering peaches in the Imperial Palace, Peking.

Maiden. The tale is taken from a series of stories called "Journeys to the West" which are popular through Chinese theater and tell of the adventures of the Monkey King, Sun Wu-kung. In this particular tale, the monk Tripitaka and Sun Wu-kung are on their way to India to find some Buddhist scriptures. They are accompanied by Sha Hsieh-sha and Chu Pa-chieh, whose name means "pig of the eight prohibitions," and the puppet of Chu is made to resemble a little fat man wearing a pig's mask or head. The eight prohibitions were imposed on Chu by the monk for the duration of the journey, one of these was that he must have nothing to do with women.

Sun Wu-kung, who could change his shape into anything he wished, decided to test Chu Pa-chieh and became a beautiful woman. Chu could not resist the lady, and placed her on his shoulders, turned around and started home. The journey was a long one. It is wittily depicted in the puppet theater by Chu trudging repeatedly across the stage, disappearing on one side and reappearing on the other, until he finally reappeared staggering, with Sun Wu-kung on his back just a few yards from his home.

Rod puppets require an entirely different kind of skill. Three rods are used, a central one attached to the head and two others joined to the wrists or elbows of the puppet arms. The central rod is concealed by the costume, but the other two are not hidden. A skilled puppeteer can make these puppets perform the trickiest of tasks such as placing a plate on the head of an acrobat puppet, or putting a bamboo yoke with dangling buckets on the shoulders of another puppet. The puppeteer often uses a little whistle called *u-dyu-dyu*, which he presses to the roof of his mouth to give his voice a high-pitched quality.

A luxurious household re-created in miniature is the setting for a puppet show in Penang, Malaysia.

The Chinese puppeteer has no greater opportunity to show his technical skills than with string puppets. Western string puppets are usually operated by eight to ten strings, whereas the movements of the Chinese puppet are controlled by up to forty and rarely less than twenty strings. These puppets can move their eyes, mouth and even eyebrows to create an astonishing range of mimicry. Unlike their Western counterparts, they can even pick up objects. European puppets only appear to pick things up by means of a piece of thread attached to the object through the palm of a puppet. As the puppet bends to touch the object, this thread is pulled tight and the object is pulled against the palm of the puppet. The little fingers of the Chinese puppet are so controlled that they can actually grip an object. There are few tasks which these puppets cannot perform, for they can paint, write, draw a sword and fight, mount a horse, ride a bicycle, perform folk dances and so on. Before the Revolution, the puppeteer had up to thirty-six different puppets to perform these tasks, but today, with an increased repertoire to include modern revolutionary themes, the cast of characters is even larger.

The string puppet theater is a simple affair, rather like a large, low table. A wood or cloth backdrop hangs across the center and the puppeteer stands behind this screen. He is concealed from the audience by another cloth that hangs in front of the stage but below the level of the top edge of the backdrop.

Young people who wished to master the craft would apprentice themselves to a master between September and March, when there was little work to be done in the fields. At the end of three such terms they would become semiprofessionals, yet it might require years of

This lively scene of puppet theater is taken from a Ming scroll painting of the sixteenth century called "The Hundred Children."

Perhaps the most haunting of all the puppet characters, these shadow puppets are made from intricately decorated, translucent animal skin. An old superstition warns that each puppet must have its head removed at night or it may cause mischief to its owner.

traveling around the country giving shows before they could begin to earn a full-time living from their skill.

Shadow puppets also originated in China and this is perhaps one of the most haunting and colorful kinds of puppetry. As with other types of puppet theater, there is a tale which tells of the beginning of shadow plays. Wu'ti, an Emperor of the Han Dynasty, was overcome by the death of his favorite concubine and requested his personal magician to summon her spirit so that he could be with her again. This the magician could not do, so after much thought he arranged a darkened room, at one end of which he placed a cloth screen, onto which he projected a colored shadow with the appearance of the dead concubine. Whatever the truth of this story there is no definite evidence that shadow plays existed much before the eighth century A.D., and even so, were not fully developed until the eleventh century.

Chinese shadow puppets are cut from the skin of an animal, which is so treated that it becomes translucent, much like parchment. Traditionally they were made from the skin of donkeys, particularly the belly skin, and from the skins of sheep, goats, water buffalo or even fish. The various parts of the shadow figure are made from different grades of skin – thicker skins for legs and arms, thinner skins for hands and the head. A design is painted onto the figure so that the colors will show when a light is shined through the skin. Nowadays, shadow puppets are usually made from plastic.

Although the shapes are usually kept fairly simple, they are decorated by cutting intricate, openwork designs into them. Each figure is usually made from twelve different pieces, the head, the body, two thighs, two lower legs, two upper and two lower arms and two hands. Each of these pieces is stitched together at one point so that they will pivot. One of the problems with translucent figures is that darker patches are created where the pieces overlap. The Chinese overcame this by cutting a wheel-like pivot where the two sections are joined. The sections are attached on alternate sides in order to keep the figure flat. The heads of the figures are designed to be interchangeable and each puppet has a collar of parchment into which the head is slipped. There is an old superstition that says that unless the head of each puppet is removed at night, it will come alive and cause great mischief to its owner. The faces are always shown in profile, stylized and painted to leave only a thin outline showing the mouth, eyes and eyebrows.

Shadow figures are worked by means of three rods, often made of thin bamboo, which are attached to the collar and to the hands by a small wire loop. The operator holds the collar rod in one hand and the two arm rods in the other. Despite the lack of controls for the legs of the figure, a skilled puppeteer has no difficulty in making them sit, walk or bend.

The shadow theater is made in several sections. The first is the screen itself, now usually made of cloth but once made from mulberry paper. The operator works behind and below this screen, at the base of which is a narrow ledge on which he can rest a puppet that he is not manipulating but which he wishes to keep in the play. Behind the puppeteer is a lantern used to cast the shadows onto the screen. Each puppet is held close to the screen so that the colors can clearly be seen on it. The effect is of a colored drawing, with clear but somewhat subdued hues.

The types of shadow puppet differ slightly in northern and southern China. Those from the North, especially Peking, are a little smaller and more delicate than those from the South, which are made of thicker leather. A red face indicates boldness and a black one indicates honesty in puppets from southern China.

The plays of the shadow theater are similar to that of other puppet theaters. Certain plays lend themselves especially well to the technique of the shadow play. "Journeys to the West" is again a popular theme with stories such as "Uproar in the Sea Kingdom" in which Sun Wu-kung wins a magic needle from the King of the Ocean, after fighting with three different-colored dragons. "Uproar in the Palace of Heaven" tells how Sun Wu-kung eats all of the Peaches of Immortality and drinks all the wine that had been prepared for a feast of the gods. Many of the plays are simple and short with very little story line, yet the skill and wit of the puppeteer in making the movements of his shadows realistic can keep his audience enthralled by improvising the story as he goes along. The performance lasts from a few minutes up to half an hour.

The theater has an important role to play in many children's toys as well, particularly in the various kinds of dolls that are popular with children, boys and girls alike. The little clay and dough figures

More comic than ferocious, a shadow puppet tiger, worked by rods, struts across the stage.

A little boy smartly turned out in his sailor suit enjoys the kindergarten playground at Schichiachuang.

Above: Whether store bought and made of clay, or homemade from dough, these charming little characters feature in many a child's makebelieve world.

Right: Dough figures like these were once sold at fairgrounds and railway stations by the poor people of Wusih.

from Wusih, now used as dolls were once made by the poor people of the town, who would sell them at fairs and railroad stations to earn extra money. The craftsmen who specialize in making these charming figures of animals and children have today been brought together in a workshop in Wusih where they continue to make these traditional toys. The clay figures, of which tigers and pandas are favorites, are painted with simple doll-like, happy faces in bright colors and are made using rubber molds and a special gypsum clay.

Similar figures are made in Chinese homes using bread dough

Bright stuffed satin toys, including the ever-popular Peking Tiger, are made for export to delight foreign children.

which is then baked. In Kwangchow, dough figures could once be bought on the streets from a "doughman" who would carry a tray of colored dough and fashion the figures for passersby. Papier-mâché dolls are now also made in Kwangchow, and clothed in elaborate costumes of embroidered silk. They are usually of legendary figures or popular theatrical characters and are often sold in sets of various characters to be used to recreate scenes from well-known plays.

Soft toys from Peking are very distinctive and much loved by children. Tigers made from cloth and stuffed with cloth remnants were once made by grandmothers as gifts for their grandchildren. These bright yellow or orange tigers are now found in many shops and are made as friendly, cuddly creatures rather than a ferocious beast. The Chinese symbol for king is always painted on the tiger's brow, for in China he is the King of Beasts. Another favorite soft toy is a black pig, decorated with red patches.

Many Chinese toys have a very long history. One of these is the shuttlecock, which is made from a coin wrapped in cloth with a few chicken feathers tied to it. In the colder parts of China, children have

Toys may change but the fascination they exert remains the same.

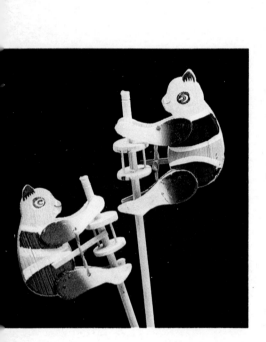

Only in recent years has the panda become a national symbol in China but the simple mechanics of these climbing bamboo toys are an age-old device.

Right: Keeping the bamboo hoop spinning around the stick requires tremendous concentration and attracts an eager and admiring audience.

devised all sorts of games to play with the shuttlecock to help them keep warm. One of the most popular is to see who can keep the shuttlecock in the air the longest using only their knees.

A great deal of skill is needed to use the diabolo, another favorite toy. The diabolo top is made from two hollow wooden wheels with intermittent slits, joined by a short axle. Children operate it by jerking two sticks connected by string which is wound once around the axle of the diabolo. When the sticks are pulled, the top runs back and forth along the string emitting a humming sound. The variations on this game are endless. Children perform all kinds of acrobatics while keeping the top spinning. Skilled players can catch the top on their string when it is thrown to them from the string of another player. These and many other traditional toys are still made in the homes of China using the natural materials such as bamboo, palm fiber, straw and even seashells.

PEKING TIGER

To make the smaller of the two Peking tigers, you will need $\frac{1}{2}$yd (0.5m) yellow cotton fabric, $\frac{1}{4}$yd (0.25m) white cotton, scraps of red and black fabric, yellow sewing thread, fabric glue, a felt tip marking pen or India ink and a fine paintbrush. The tiger is stuffed with one pound (0.5kg) of sawdust, which makes the toy very firm and solid. Before using the sawdust, bake it in a medium oven for an hour to sterilize it. Pack the sawdust firmly into the body. To make a softer toy, stuff the tiger with kapok or foam chips.

First cut out all the pattern pieces and begin by pinning the two body pieces and the belly right sides together. Baste and machine stitch firmly leaving an opening at the tail end of the spine for stuffing. Sew up the center seam of tail, stuff the tail and fold under raw edges at base. Slip stitch the tail to the body. Sew ears as shown on page 42, poke holes indicated in the head with scissors, push ears through and secure from the inside. Stuff the body firmly and stitch up the opening left at the base of the spine.

The Peking tiger is decorated with the Chinese character that means "king," because in the East the tiger is the king of beasts.

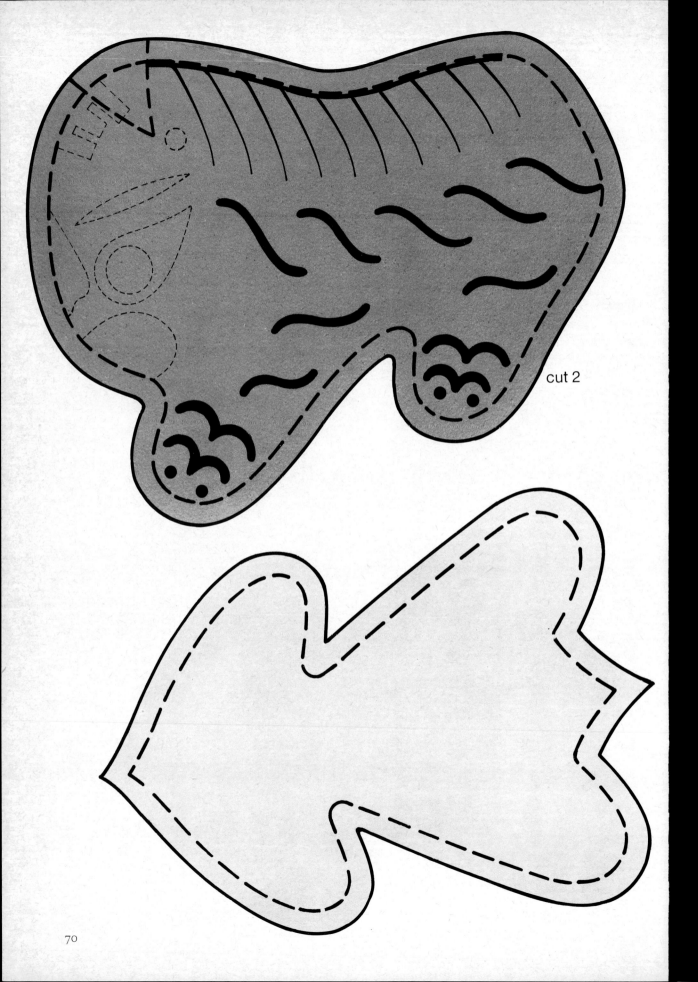

cut 2

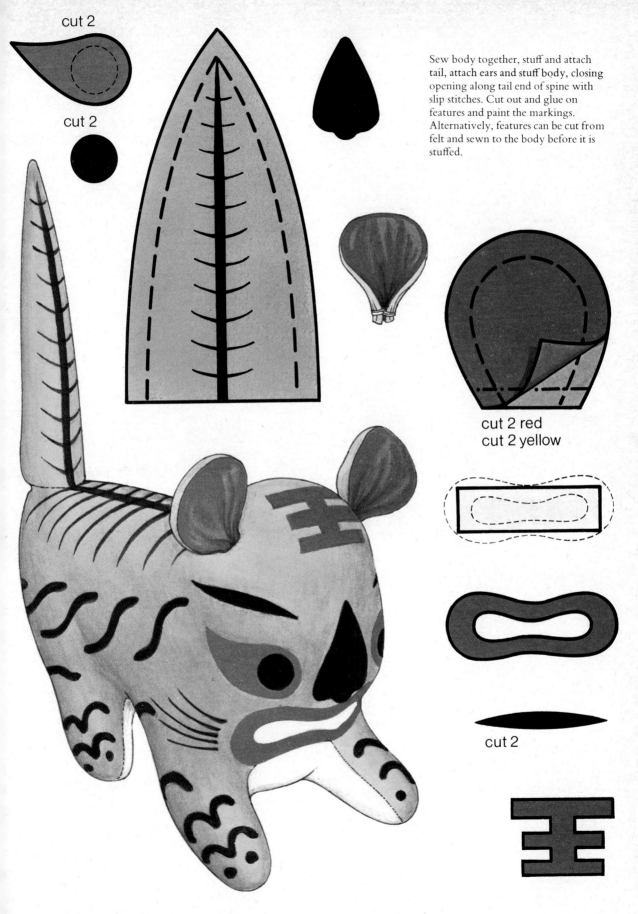

cut 2

cut 2

Sew body together, stuff and attach tail, attach ears and stuff body, closing opening along tail end of spine with slip stitches. Cut out and glue on features and paint the markings. Alternatively, features can be cut from felt and sewn to the body before it is stuffed.

cut 2 red
cut 2 yellow

cut 2

71

WUSIH DOUGH FIGURES

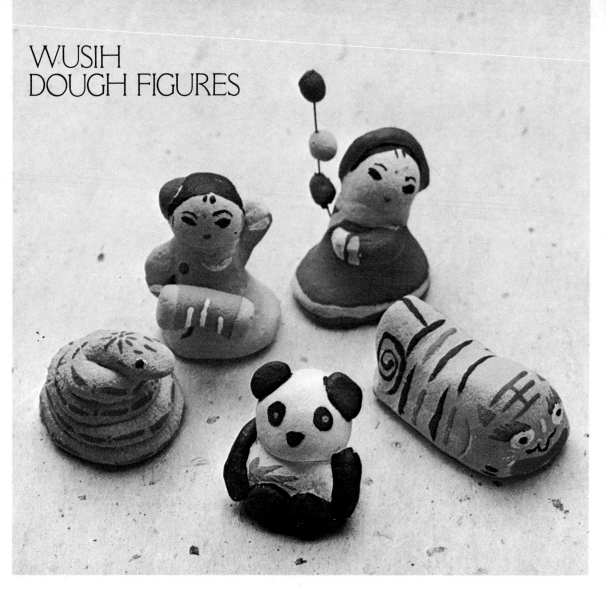

A fat panda, Peking tiger, coiled snake and costumed dancers all made of dough, form a charming array of miniature figures that are traditional toys of China.

These delightful, brightly painted dough figures are usually stylized forms of animals and dancers in costume and plump babies simply shaped in colored dough with expressive painted details.

All the ingredients needed to make these charming dough figures can be found in any kitchen. The dough, made from equal parts of plain flour and salt mixed with water, is a clean and workable modeling material. It is cheap enough to be made in large quantities and if any dough is left over after a modeling session, it can be stored in a plastic bag in the refrigerator until it is needed. The dough is tinted with drops of food coloring to the shade desired before you start modeling. When the figures are shaped, they are then baked in a cool oven until they are hard. It is important to keep the temperature low and to check the figures frequently so that they do not brown. If they begin to brown, turn down the oven temperature. The dough figures are then painted with poster, enamel or acrylic paints and varnished so that they stay hard.

Materials: Plain flour, salt, water, measuring cup, mixing bowl, pastry board, baking sheet, food coloring in red, yellow and blue, poster or acrylic paints in black, white, green, red, blue, yellow and purple, gold and silver enamel paints, fine paintbrush, short lengths of thin wire.

The basic modeling dough is made from equal quantities of flour and salt, mixed with just enough water to form a firm dough. Knead the dough for 20 minutes to mix all the ingredients thoroughly. One cup each of flour and salt will produce enough dough to make all the figures shown here.

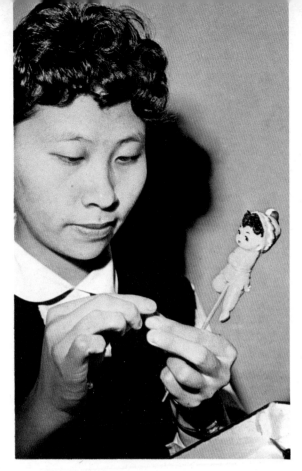

Dough figures are today made in many provinces of China. They are produced in workshops and sold in shops as well as being made by a traveling "dough man" who sets up a stand in the city streets and fashions lively figures from an array of brightly colored dough which he carries with him. The dough man is a great attraction and children gather around him as his nimble fingers shape tiny bits of colored clay into the details of a doll-like figure or animal shape. These figures are set out in the sun to dry rather than baking them in an oven.

After kneading the dough, divide it into quarters. Leave one quarter white to use for the panda body and knead food coloring into the other quarters. Add red and yellow to make orange for the tiger, red and blue to make purple for the snake, and red to make pink for the dancers.

When the coloring has been thoroughly kneaded into the dough, begin modeling the figures. Heads, limbs and ears can be stuck onto the body by slightly wetting both surfaces to be joined. Details such as the dancer's drum and staff are attached to the bodies with short lengths of wire.

Indent the base of each figure so that it stays flat during baking. Bake the figures for three to four hours starting them at 300°F (150°C) and reducing the heat to 225°F (110°C) after the first hour. If the oven is too hot, the figures will turn brown so check frequently.

When the figures have been thoroughly dried and hardened by baking, allow them to cool and then paint on all the details and features following our photographs as a guide. The figures are then painted with two coats of clear varnish to preserve them and make them waterproof.

Opposite: This eighteenth century print by Hua Ching Lei from an album of manners shows the doughman at work.

CHAPTER 6
PRECIOUS LACQUERS AND JEWELED ENAMELS

Throughout the provinces of central and southern China grows a tree whose sap has been the source of a uniquely Chinese craft for some three thousand years. The lac tree, or to use its correct name, *Rhus vernicifera*, exudes a resin that has remarkable properties. A Jesuit missionary writing from Peking in 1685 was particularly enthusiastic about the lacquerware he found there.

"Besides the brightness and luster which is the property of varnish, it hath moreover a certain quality of preserving the wood upon which it is applied, especially as they do not mix any other matter with it. Worms do not easily breed in it, nay, and moisture scarcely ever penetrates it, not so much as any scent can fasten to it; if during meals there be any Grease or Potage spilled, if it presently be wiped with a wet Clout, one not only finds no remainders or sign of it, but does not so much as perceive the least smell."

With properties such as these it is not surprising that the first use of lacquer was as a protective coating. In fact, it seems to have been used in this way on an astounding number of objects, from wood, pottery and porcelain to silk hats, leather shoes and even to coat little duck-shaped baskets woven from bamboo.

Utensils were made from lacquer at least two thousand years ago, using a simple technique. A piece of cloth soaked in lacquer was molded around a wooden model of, say, a cup or dish. After the lacquer had dried, the model was lifted out from the hardened lacquer and cloth "skin." This skin was then coated with further layers of lacquer until the vessel was hard enough to stand daily use. This was the primitive beginnings of a craft that now requires a high degree of skill, for the Chinese learned not only to decorate their lacquerwork but to apply enough layers of lacquer to be able to carve the surface.

The lacquer itself, called *ch'i*, is tapped in the summer from lac

This impressive carved lacquer Kwan Yin vase is decorated with flower and bird motifs.

Opposite: The individual wire cells on the body of a cloisonné vase are filled with enamel by a craftsman at the Arts and Crafts Factory in Peking.

The process of lacquering has changed little over the centuries. This craftsman in a nineteenth century print carves a design in lacquer in the same way as today's artisans.

This lustrously colored lacquer vase is typical of the wares produced for export by Chinese crafts workshops.

trees that are about ten years old. Horizontal incisions are made in the trunk from the base of the tree upward in groups, alternatively left to right. Branches more than about one inch thick are also tapped. The sap is very poisonous, however, causing rashes and blisters and it is dangerous to inhale the fumes. Those who work the trees must wear some kind of protective clothing. In earlier times this was a linen hood tied at the neck with cord with two tiny eye slits as the only openings. Today workers wear industrial masks to protect their faces. The sap is collected in small cups or sometimes allowed to run into a hollow bamboo tube, which reduces the danger to the workers. The tapping process kills the tree, though new shoots appear quickly from the root, which is left in the ground.

The resin is grayish-white at first but soon darkens. It is strained through hemp cloth to remove any pieces of wood. It is then placed in shallow wooden tubs and stirred out in the sunshine or over a slow burning fire to remove excess moisture and bring it to a uniform consistency. Except for adding coloring, the lacquer is now ready for use and is sealed in large airtight containers. Lacquer at this stage is a dark, reddish-brown. The two most common colors of Chinese lacquerware are red and black, produced by adding iron sulfate for black, and cinnabar, an ore of mercury, for red to the natural lacquer. White, green and yellow lacquers can be made using lead, chromium and cadmium pigments.

The making of the best painted lacquerwork is a long and painstaking task that can take as long today as it did two thousand years ago, for the secret lies in the long drying of each layer of lacquer. The base to which the lacquer is applied, whether it is a tray, vase, bowl, cabinet or chair, is usually made of wood. Metal and pottery have been used occasionally for smaller objects. Favorite woods include pine, willow and camphor, chosen for their soft and even grain. When the wood base has been finished its surface is carefully sanded, and cracks and joins filled in with a mixture which was once made from rice paste and lacquer. The surface is then carefully smoothed again.

The wood is now ready for priming by the application of two coats of lacquer. Each is allowed to dry for at least a day to let it sink into the wood. Lacquer dries best in a dark place and in a humid atmosphere, for it is the moisture in the air that makes for successful slow drying. The primed wood is now covered with a layer of hemp cloth, cotton or paper. In the finest work, silk is used. The cloth is first soaked in raw lacquer and smoothed to fit the contours of the wood, allowed to dry and ground to an even surface. Successive layers of lacquer are then applied and each is allowed to dry for up to a week before the next layer is put on. The work is tedious, for each layer of lacquer is only the thickness of a coat of paint and much of this is removed by the grinding.

Once the lacquering is complete, the piece passes into the hands of the painter, or *hua kang*. The colors he uses are also made from lacquer prepared in a much wider variety of colors than the lacquer base. Turquoise and slate-blue, wine-red and rose-red, white, dark purple and plum are frequently used colors made by adding various pigments to lacquer. The painter today works with brushes of horsehair, although once they were made from wild pig and rat's hair. When the painting is finished, the whole work is covered with a thin coat of clear lacquer.

Painted Chinese lacquerwork, masterfully executed, has a beauty of its own. The favorite color for backgrounds is black, which gives a luminous quality to the painted design. Each dynasty had its own

This close-up of classic carved lacquer work on sale at the Kwangchow Trade Fair shows great craftsmanship.

Old Masters train the new apprentices in the skills of carving lacquer at the Peking Arts and Crafts Factory. More than 50 per cent of the workers at the factory are women.

preferences for designs shown in the lacquerwork produced in the Imperial factories or workshops. The lacquerwork of modern China reflects the two thousand years of design it has to call upon. The favorite motif of the Han craftsman was the cloud scroll, which symbolizes the misty, towering landscapes loved by the Taoists. Birds and flowers are often painted together – the pheasant and the peony are both emblems of beauty, love and affection. The stork and the pine always go together as symbols of long life. The bamboo, pine and flowering plum are often grouped as the three friends because they keep green in cold weather.

Lacquer has been inlaid with gold and silver foil, mother-of-pearl and tortoiseshell since it first became a skilled craft from the time of the T'ang emperors. This intricate inlaywork added a new dimension to the effects that could be achieved with lacquer. By the time of the T'ang emperors, however, a new lacquerwork was fast gaining popularity. No longer was the craftsman simply painting, inlaying or even incising his lacquers. He had discovered that there was virtually no end to the number of coats of lacquer he could apply to a piece. The end result was lacquer so thick that it could be carved.

The method for carved lacquer is much the same as for the preparation of lacquer to be painted except that up to two hundred layers are applied on the base. As before, a period of a week may pass between successive coats, and a large piece may take two years before it is ready to be carved. The final wall of lacquer is sometimes over half an inch thick. The last layer is the most important, and a special refined lacquer is used for this. The piece is then placed in a dust-free room at the correct temperature and humidity for a week.

The carving must be done while the lacquer is still soft enough to be cut cleanly with a sharp knife. The craftsman has a number of knives with varying shaped blades for use in different designs. These knives must be kept extremely sharp and must be well-controlled in use, for the slightest slip can mean weeks of repair work. Sometimes

Top: Smooth lacquerware can be formed into elegant shapes, such as this vase, and painted in subtle colors.

Carved lacquer is formed into many shapes; vases, screens and bowls such as the one pictured above.

Right: These beads are carved in traditional red lacquer and incised with stylized Chinese characters.

two or more colors are used in the lacquering and then the top color is carved away to expose the color underneath. In this variation, each layer of color must be placed at exactly the right depth and each must be of the same thickness.

The final polishing in all lacquerwork is done with fine-textured slate powders which are applied with the palm of the hand. The result is the brilliancy found in glazed porcelain or enamel.

As the popularity of Chinese lacquerware spread to Europe in the nineteenth and twentieth centuries, the craftsman often found it difficult to keep up with the delivery dates demanded by his foreign buyers. As a result, some craftsmen used a shortcut method that is not considered true practice of the craft by the best artisans. Instead of waiting for each of the many coats of lacquer to dry, the shape would be formed around wood using a special putty made from plaster and raw lacquer. Once this base was prepared it would be covered with only a few coats of colored lacquer. An even shorter method was simply to paint several layers of lacquer over a carved wooden base. Today, the time honored techniques of lacquerwork are again being practiced in crafts workshops all over China.

The Chinese are past masters at adapting new methods in crafts to suit their particular style. In cloisonné, they have taken a technique not their own and produced a purely Chinese style. Cloisonné was learned from the Arabs during the time of Marco Polo and Kublai Khan and within a few years workshops had been set up in Peking.

Cloisonné is a technique used for decorating surfaces with enamels contained in cells of fine wirework, so that the colors do not run together. With this technique, the most elaborate and delicate patterns can be obtained. The craft, even as practiced in Peking today, requires a number of skills, and apprentices will usually specialize in one of them. Vases, jars, boxes, incense burners and large dishes, even little animal figures and strings of beads, are some of the shapes that the craftsman has chosen to decorate with the intricate, mosaiclike patterns of cloisonné.

The body onto which the wires are fixed is usually made of metal, either cast in bronze or built from sheets of copper. The sheets are hammered into shape and soldered together, and even complicated

Fine, pointed tools are used by the craftsman to cut away areas of lacquer to form the desired pattern.

Cloisonné is made so fine that it is impossible to distinguish the individual cells of color on the surface of a piece. This lovely vase displays a phoenix amidst birds.

A highly skilled and experienced craftsman applies copper wire to a brass base to form cloisons, or cells, to enclose the enamel.

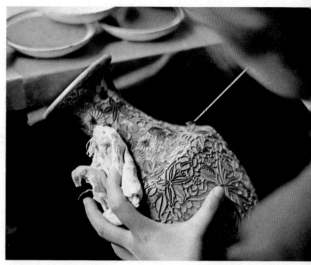

Top and above: Workers at the Arts and Crafts Factory in Peking choose from a bright array of enamels and carefully fill each wire-formed cell with liquid color. This is done with a tiny ladle or with a tool that acts like an eye-dropper. The cloisonné ware is then fired so that the enamel fuses with the metal surface of the base.

shapes can be made in this way. Attaching the wires to form individual cells to hold the enamel is a close and delicate task. In Peking today, the design is first drawn on the copper base, often from memory if the artisan has had many years of experience. The workman then forms fine, flat copper wires to follow the lines of the design. The method of attaching the wires can vary, but must be performed with care and attention to make sure that each wire touches another to form completely enclosed cells. If gaps are left, one enamel color may flow into another. In one method the copper base is coated with a thin layer of clear or colored enamel and fired. The formed wire is then put into position on the surface and held with a thin gum solution. The piece is then refired and the wire is embedded in the enamel. With a faster method, the wires are placed onto the clean metal, also with a gum solution, and enamel powder is sprinkled over the whole surface and the piece is then fired.

The intricate wire cells or "cloisons" are now ready to be filled with various colored enamels according to the design. It is in the compounding and mixing of these colors that the Chinese cloisonné workers have given this old craft new style. A basic enamel is a mixture of flint, lead oxide or sand, with soda or potash. These are the same materials as found in ordinary glass. They are colored by the addition of small amounts of metal oxides, and the shades of even one color depends on the whole enamel mixture.

The beautiful blues that are frequently used in Chinese cloisonné eluded would-be copiers for centuries until it was discovered that the basic Chinese enamel contained no lead oxide. The presence of this substance seemed to prevent certain shades of blue from developing during firing. It was not only chance, however, that gave the Chinese craftsman an unusual choice of colors. From the fifteenth century, they have used a method called "mixed colors." For normal use, enamel powder, as fine as possible, is mixed to a paste with water. For mixed colors, fairly large granules of two different colors of enamel are mixed and fused to give an intermediate shade, which is hard to define even on close examination. The first of these mixed colors was Ming Pink made by mingling granules of red and white. The mixture of colors used for this method today is much finer and the fragments are so finely divided that the gradation of color is extremely subtle.

The motifs used in cloisonné have varied over the centuries from simple floral patterns of lotus, pomegranates and peony scrolls, to the crowded yet intricate patterns of the Ch'ing, many of which are skillfully copied today. The dragon, phoenix, mandarin ducks, and Dogs of *Fo*, the guardians of Buddhist temples, have all gained new dimensions and life through being portrayed in cloisonné. Even with such complex designs the most skilled pieces show no trace of the cells that make up the pattern.

Another method of combining enamel and metalwork is painted enamel on copper, called *yang-tz'u*, which literally means "foreign porcelain." This technique was introduced to China during the reign of K'ang Hsi from 1662 to 1722 by French missionaries from their knowledge of Limoges enamels. The surface of the copper is coated with an opaque enamel onto which the design is painted in enamel colors. The Chinese accepted this kind of enamel work only for export products and many of the things made were therefore decorated with European subjects rather than traditional Chinese motifs. The prettiest of these designs are teapots and cups with landscapes in blue enamel on a white background.

Delicate and stylized floral patterns cover these modern cloisonné beads.

Above: Cloisonné ware is formed into many fanciful shapes such as this tripon.

Left: Cloisonné vases made at the Peking Arts and Crafts Factory are closely inspected before being carefully packed and shipped to many parts of the world.

CHAPTER 7
PLANT OF A THOUSAND USES

Throughout southern China as far north as the Yangtze River groves of bamboo are found almost everywhere, on mountainsides, flat-lands, riverbanks and around houses. It is sometimes hard to believe that this tough, woody plant, often reaching a height of over one hundred feet, is in fact a grass and not a tree. Bamboo grows very rapidly and the new shoots put out by a mature plant toward the end of winter grow to their full height in less than a season. In the best conditions such as those existing in Kiangsi Province with its temperate climate and plentiful rainfall, bamboo can grow two feet in under forty-eight hours.

There are probably few plants that have been put to as many uses as bamboo. Fences, water pipes, tool handles, walking sticks, furniture, fishing rods, drinking cups, woven mats and cooking utensils are all made of bamboo. The split stem is crafted into mats, baskets, hats, chairs, stools, fans, chopsticks and umbrella frames. The many varieties of bamboo lend themselves to particular uses. Fine grained pole is steamed into shapes to make graceful furniture, while mottled bamboo and water bamboo is split into thin threads for weaving. A thick bamboo is used to make flat boards to support heavy weights and so is useful in constructing beds and work tables.

Before the Revolution there was little deliberate cultivation of bamboo in southern China, and supplies in some areas were dwindling rapidly. Since then there has been extensive cultivation in Kiangsi Province and as a result, new handicraft centers are springing up. Some towns, such as Hokon, have been bamboo handicraft centers since the seventeenth century and the now plentiful supply of raw material has made them active once again.

With only a few simple tools, often made by the craftsman himself, sturdy and attractive furniture is made in small, communal workshops. The craftsman buys his bamboo in whole stems which

Cut lengths of bamboo are stacked ready for a variety of uses.

Opposite: Brightly painted paper parasols have been known in China since the fourth century and are very popular among country people.

Before the Revolution there was little deliberate cultivation of bamboo, but now there are many groves, especially in Kiangsi Province.

Bamboo furniture is strong but light in weight. Below: A craftsman in Changsha puts the finishing touches to a simple but sturdy bed while, below right, a nineteenth century trades album shows a more elaborate piece of furniture being made.

he saws into convenient lengths with a bow-shaped saw with a bamboo handle. The chairs made from these whole bamboo sections are smaller than ordinary chairs and look like children's furniture. The technique for making them seems disarmingly simple. Two lengths of bamboo, about two inches in diameter, are bent at right angles in two places, forming U-shapes. To do this, sections are cut out of the tube where it is to be bent leaving only a strip of bamboo wall on one side. The strip sections are then held over a fire and gradually bent to a right angle. The heat makes the bamboo flexible. Two shorter and narrower tubes are then fitted into the bends of the U-shaped sections and secured with nails. This is the basic frame of

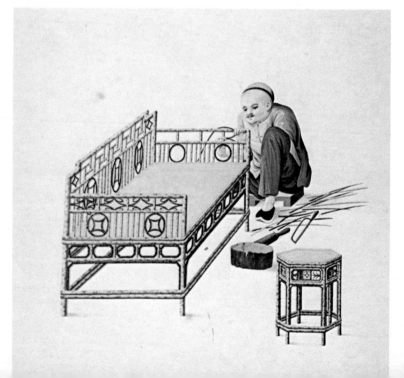

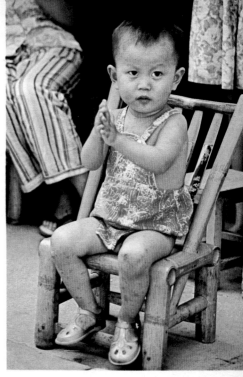

the chair. Rungs of tubing are fitted between the legs to add stability and the seat of slatted bamboo is attached.

In many cases the craftsman needs to use pieces of split bamboo for his various crafts, rather than the whole tube. A special knife with a curved end, somewhat like a cheese knife, but with a razor sharp edge is used for this purpose. A length of bamboo tubing is placed upright on the ground and the knife is pressed downward into the

Left: Before he can weave his baskets the craftsman must split the bamboo into finer lengths using a special hatchetlike knife.

Above: Adults as well as children find these small, simply made bamboo chairs comfortable.

The traditional "coolie" hat is made from thin strips of closely woven bamboo, as shown in this nineteenth century print.

Light and airy, this delicate bird cage is made from strips of split bamboo and decorated with carved bamboo medallions.

tube. Once the initial cut has been made, the splitting proceeds easily, for the knife has a triangular cross section that acts as a wedge. The "nose" of the knife prevents the blade from touching the ground and blunting. Thin, square sectioned strips are cut in this way and are used for making such items as delicate, many-tiered bird cages.

Very thin strips or splints of bamboo, used for weaving, are shaved from lengths of tube using a tool similar to a woodworking plane, which has several sizes of blades. The traditional "coolie" hat is made from these splints sometimes woven over a thick layer of dry, sheathlike leaves to make the hat rainproof.

Infinitely versatile, bamboo is crafted into things as diverse as this pretty trinket box and the wide brimmed hats that shield the field worker against sun and rain.

Left, and below: In old China fans were an important part of daily life. Now they are made chiefly for export.

Bamboo can be shaved so finely that threads are all that remain. The craftsmen of Hokon in Kiangsi Province today use these threads to weave tiny toy figures of pheasants, frogs, ducks and chickens. Miniature wooden boxes are covered with delicate bamboo strips dyed in bright colors and laid out in complex geometrical designs. Considerable skill is needed both for shaving bamboo threads and for this intricate bamboo mosaic work, in which as many as forty threads are used to decorate a square inch.

Folding fans are made in bamboo crafts centers using split bamboo for the frame which is then covered with paper or silk. Fans have been popular in China since ancient times and are made in two basic styles; folding and fixed fans. Ornately decorated fans are now made in China only for export, though they were once an important part of daily life. They were used not only to give a cooling current of

Above: A variety of traditionally styled fixed fans. Below: A modern folding fan.

Silk parasols are a famous product of Hangchow. In recent years the Hungchi workshop there has introduced many new and lively designs to add to the range of traditional patterns.

The hot springs near Sian, once the capital of the T'ang Dynasty, are now a popular fun palace.

air but also to emphasize points of speech by gesturing in the air or to mark out Chinese characters in the air when the spoken word was not understood.

At one time it was fashionable to have different fans for men and women. A man's fan contained either nine, sixteen, twenty or twenty-four ribs while a woman's fan had not less than thirty ribs. Similarly, feminine figures could be used to decorate women's fans but not a man's. It was also fashionable, particularly among the rich, to have a different fan for each season of the year. The fan is the emblem of Chung-li Ch'uan, one of the Eight Taoist Immortals and it is said that he was able to revive the dead by a wave of his fan.

Parasols made from bamboo and oiled paper first appeared in the fourth century A.D., though silk parasols were known long before that. The parasol is one of the Eight Auspicious Signs on the Sole of the Buddha's Foot and a parasol called the Umbrella of Ten Thousand People used to be presented to a popular official when he left his district to take up another post. It was a token of respect and purity and a symbol of dignity and was inscribed with the names of the donors in gold letters.

Inexpensive parasols were later made from rag paper while the more expensive ones used a particularly strong paper made from the bark of a mulberry tree. The bark of the mulberry was mixed with a little bamboo bark, chalk, rice stubble and water, then boiled for several hours to form a paste from which the sheets of paper were made. The paper parasols were painted with letters, landscapes and flowers in bright colors, and then lacquered with a thin coating of clear or slightly tinted lacquer. Some parasols have up to forty-two ribs made from split bamboo. Painted silk parasols with bamboo ribs are still made in Hangchow and oiled paper parasols usually painted yellow or bright red are made in many parts of the country. These umbrellas are popular with people in rural areas.

Far left: With the addition of a handle, a cup is easily made from a section of bamboo. Left: Split bamboo is woven into sleeping mats while even finer strands are used to weave ingenious and decorative containers, such as this duck basket.

With an increasing demand for bamboo crafts, the workers of Kiangsi have developed an increasing range of products. One of these uses two craft techniques, lacquering and bamboo weaving. Lacquer forms are built around clay molds and bamboo is woven over the lacquer forms in the shape of ducks and chickens. These are frequently used as containers for cookies and candy. Bamboo cups are made in great quantities. These cups are simply made by sawing a bamboo stem just below a knot where the bamboo stem is solid and again about six inches above the knot. The edges are trimmed and rounded and the surface polished to finish the cup.

Not surprisingly, the people of the province find a huge variety of uses for bamboo in their homes; bamboo mats to sleep on, pillows stuffed with bamboo shavings, roll-down bamboo blinds and slatted bamboo containers in which to steam dumplings. Small outbuildings have roofs made from lengths of bamboo tubing split down the middle creating a corrugated effect and these same sections make admirable guttering pipes. Even pegs for building are made from bamboo and bamboo cow bells are hung with wooden clappers.

Every Chinese home has several of these bamboo steamers.

Skillful fingers weave rattan cane, from the climbing rattan palm, into a variety of useful objects at the Ting Chow commune rattan factory near Kwangchow.

Woven bamboo containers fulfill myriad uses in the Chinese household.

Craftswomen at the Tailen Shell Workshop carefully select and arrange the carved shells for a new picture.

A contemporary basket of intricate and decoratively woven bamboo.

The bamboo handicraft industry is flourishing in China today, and a great diversity of products is made both for use in China and for export. The array of bamboo ware available ranges from fairly simple furniture and steamers for the kitchen to tiny bamboo toys and whistles and incredibly fine basketware made of braided or woven strips of bamboo. The material is often left in its natural color and simply coated with shellac to make it shiny.

A technique similar to that used for making little bamboo mosaic figures, is used in Swatow, in Kwangtung Province, to make tiny pictures pieced together in colored wheat straw. At Harbin, in Heilungkiang Province, the craftsmen have extended this idea and now make these pictures so that they appear three-dimensional. The threads of wheat straw are so delicate and subtly shaded that when they are pieced together they can be made to look like the fur of a squirrel or the feathers of a bird. These collages are also made using feathers, dyed and cut into shapes, or pieces of fur.

Mosaic techniques are also used to make collages from carved shells, a craft which began in Lushun about fourteen years ago. Shells

Left and below: Shell and feather collages, such as these on exhibition at the Kwangchow Trade Fair, are sold all over the world.

from the coasts around Lushun are collected, carved and gradually built up into collages of flowers, birds, landscapes and people. A picture of the design to be followed is first painted on a silk background, then pieces of shell are selected according to their color, texture and shape and fixed onto the background following the contours of the design. When the work is finished, a coat of varnish is applied to the whole work. The craft requires great patience, care and an understanding of the thousands of different varieties of shell that are available. Shell collages are now made mainly in Nanking.

A girl working in a crafts center delicately pieces together feathers to make birds for a collage picture.

93

STRAW MOSAIC

The grain and attractive sheen of straw make it a very decorative material. The Chinese use colored straw to make tiny collage pictures and to decorate small wooden boxes with astonishingly intricate patterns. Straws dyed in bright colors can be bought from craft shops. Unfortunately, it is difficult to achieve bright, even color by dyeing straw at home. However, the natural color of straw is attractive in itself and beautiful patterns can be made by laying the undyed straw in different directions and at different angles. The straw must be flattened before it can be used for mosaic work. First, each straw is slit down one side with a razor blade or sharp craft knife. The straws are soaked in warm water for at least two hours. After soaking they are pressed flat with a hot iron and are ready for use. Looking at a Chinese box decorated in straw mosaic, it appears as if each tiny piece of straw has been individually and painstakingly glued down. However, the process becomes extremely simple if the flat ribbons of straw are first glued side by side onto a piece of paper to make a whole sheet of straw. The straw and paper can then be cut into all sorts of shapes, squares, diamonds or thin strips and then arranged into a pattern and glued onto a box to make an endless variety of geometric patterns.

Decorative cards with straw arranged in patterns to form birds and flowers and landscapes make attractive and personal greeting cards, gift tags and bookmarks.

94

Straw collage

The secret of making tiny straw collage pictures is to outline each separate section of the collage on tracing paper, glue straw onto the paper and then cut out each part of the design following the traced outline. Even flattened straw retains a slight curve so when gluing it to paper, hammer it flat with a mallet until the glue is completely dry. The straw and paper can then be treated as one when making either a collage or a mosaic. The only materials required for straw collage are colored straws, an iron, glue, scissors and a razor blade or craft knife, an appropriate weight paper and paint to color in the background if necessary.

Each straw must be slit before it is soaked. Stand the straw up and with a razor blade or sharp knife, make a slit in the straw down one side from top to bottom.

After slitting each straw, soak all the straws in warm water for at least two hours. After soaking thoroughly, shake off the water and iron each straw flat using a hot iron.

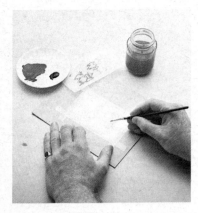

Make a tracing of the design. Rub a
soft pencil over the back of the tracing
and lightly transfer the design to the
paper. Paint in any background sky
or water in the design.

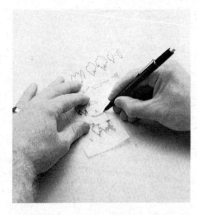

On a separate piece of tracing paper
outline each part of the design, each
separate leaf, branch, part of a house,
etc. These tracings form the patterns
for the straw shapes.

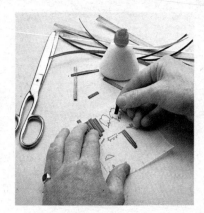

Cut the straw into short lengths and
glue it down over the tracings. Press
the straw down firmly; hammering
it flat ensures that it is thoroughly
stuck down.

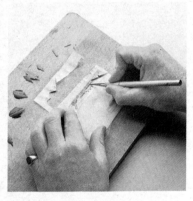

When the glue is dry, cut out each
straw shape following the traced outline on the back. Use either scissors or
a craft knife, whichever feels most
comfortable.

Following the outline, lightly drawn
on the background paper, stick down
each piece of straw to form the design.
Glue the branches first, overlapping
the foliage slightly on top.

Make sure each piece of straw is
firmly stuck down, then mount the
collage on a piece of cardboard or
colored paper to make a greeting card
or bookmark.

Choose the background paper of the
cards to look attractive with the colors
of straw that you are using and the
pattern which is being made. Black
contrasts with pastel straw colors.

Kwangtung
straw box

This tiny box is intricately decorated with bright slivers of straw, which form a complex geometric design.

On graph paper, draw a plan to the exact size of the box, including sides as well as the top. Draw in the exact outlines of the design, plan colors and directions of each straw section. This plan can then be cut up and the pieces used as patterns for the straw mosaic.

The half-finished box shows pattern pieces cut from graph paper, sheets of straw and the mosaic pattern arranged on the box. Cover one complete side at a time, holding the lid on tightly with masking tape. When the glue is dry, slit the straw between the box lid and base and begin work on another side of the box.

This decorative selection of straw mosaic boxes shows the versatility of this craft method.

Cover a sheet of paper with straws glued side by side. Hammer the straw absolutely flat onto the paper. When the glue is dry, straw and paper can be treated as one and cut out into tiny shapes to be re-arranged into the mosaic pattern of your choice.

Straws glued onto a sheet of paper can be cut into strips and re-arranged into the most intricate and beautiful mosaiclike patterns.

CHAPTER 8
CARPETS FIT FOR AN EMPEROR

A full scale working drawing of a carpet pattern is drawn up from an artist's original design.

Opposite: On a modern silk rug, a magnificent dragon, chasing the sacred pearl, sinuously winds itself around a pillar.

"That so many of the poor should suffer from cold,
What can we do to prevent it?
To bring warmth to a single body is not much use.
I wish I had a big rug ten thousand feet long,
Which, at one time, could cover up every inch of the city."
"The Big Rug" Po Chii-I (772–846)

In many of the houses of North China an essential feature of the home is a *k'ang*, a large, heated brick platform on which the family sleep. During the day, however, their cotton mattresses are folded away and the family carpet is laid on top of the k'ang to make a comfortable place to sit. Since the k'ang is a central feature of a house the best carpet is used to cover it.

Carpets have never been used solely as decorative floor coverings in China. In addition to covering the k'ang, they are often used as wall hangings partly to keep the room warmer. Many of the symbolic motifs used on carpets dictated where they would be placed in the home. Carpets with patterns that converge on the center were always placed on the floor, while those with other patterns were used as wall hangings. Many Chinese homes did not have chairs, so that carpets were even more important in providing comfort. The design and color of Chinese carpets reflects this importance and it has been said that a room with only a stool and a Chinese carpet can appear fully furnished.

The craft of carpet making did not originate in China but probably first came from India or Persia. Nevertheless as with other techniques learned from foreign peoples, the Chinese have adapted carpet making to create a purely Chinese style. Sadly, no actual examples of knotted carpets made before the seventeenth century remain, though we know from Chinese literature that they were

The pile of the finished carpet is clipped to emboss the surface and emphasize the beauty of the whole design.

A small rug woven in glowing many-colored hues.

being made much earlier. The history of the carpets can be divided into two phases, distinguished by an increasing use of chemical dyes toward the end of the nineteenth century.

Until the middle of the last century one of the most appealing characteristics of Chinese carpets was the unsurpassed, subtle use of colors. The use of color was often so restrained that only two colors were used on a carpet. Blue is the favorite color of Chinese carpets particularly a dark, luminous blue which is a unique Chinese achievement. The shades of blue are used mainly for the patterns and only rarely used as background. This may be because the blues, which were made from the vegetable dye indigo, faded much less easily than other colors.

When the pattern is blue, the background colors most favored are brown, off-white and a special red called fruit-red. Fruit-red, unlike most other shades of red, has no blue in it, and it mellows into superb hues. Sometimes yellow wool would be dyed with this red, giving a shade, which as the carpet aged, gained great depth and beauty. The Chinese preferred to use natural browns like those of camel or sheep wool, though both of these wools were dyed brown to help them retain their color.

Yellow was the Imperial color, and pure, luxurious yellow was reserved especially for the use of the court. Other shades of yellow used outside the court, ranged from pale yellow, honey and amber to orange. Colors as bright as lemon yellow were not used before the nineteenth century, and shades like chartreuse are modern colors and are not as pleasing and harmonious as the subtle, traditional shades.

The invention of chemical aniline dyes completely changed the quality of colors, for unlike vegetable dyes, these chemicals destroy the sheen and oil of the wool, making it stiff, dry and hard. Chemical dyes produce none of the soft modulations of color possible with vegetable dyes. More recent advances in the use of chemical dyes has made some progress in restoring the qualities lost.

The shape of the loom used for knotting rugs has not changed for centuries, only the materials used in its construction have altered. The loom was originally a strong, wooden frame of four beams set at right-angles to each other. In looms used today, the vertical beams are anchored to the floor and the horizontal beams are movable. The warp is tied vertically across the horizontal beams. The warp threads are kept tight by the lower beam, which hangs loosely. The carpet makers sit on narrow wooden planks hanging from ropes in front of the warp. And several workers can work on the same carpet at one time. Hanging within their reach are balls of wool that are unwound and tied with special knots around one or two warp threads. The warp is knotted in horizontal rows from the bottom upward and when each row of horizontal knots is completed, it is secured with up to four cotton weft threads. The number of knots in a row can easily be counted from the back of the carpet. Since the number of vertical knots is less easy to count, the finished carpet is weighed to assess the total number of knots to determine the amount of wool that has gone into the carpet and the price it will cost, based on the work involved and the cost of materials.

As the rug is knotted, the plank on which the workers sit is raised upward. If the loom is smaller than the required carpet size, the finished section is drawn back around the lower beam and new warp threads are spliced onto the original ones.

The carpets at the Number 1 carpet factory in Tientsin are all hand knotted.

Another carpet grows beneath the skillful fingers of the workers at the Tientsin factory. Of the 1,300 employees, 57 per cent are women.

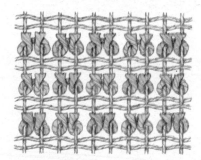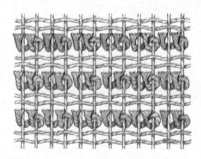

The Persian and Turkish knot are used in making traditional Chinese carpets.

The outline of the carpet design is drawn onto the warp threads for the weavers to follow.

Electric shears make the work of embossing the carpet pile much faster and easier than the methods used in the past.

The knots traditionally used in Chinese carpets are the Persian or Sehna knot and the Turkish or Ghiordes knot. The latter is frequently used at the ends of each row as it provides a firmer edge to the carpet. The Chinese use thicker wool for the knotting, creating a deeper pile than is found in Persian carpets. At the same time, because each row of knots is interspersed with up to four, heavy weft threads, a slanted effect is achieved in the pile.

Embossing and incising are two techniques that the carpet maker uses to considerable effect. Embossing is achieved by knotting the carpet on two levels with the knots of the background cut shorter than the knots of the pattern or vice versa. Incising is a method used on the finished carpet. It is either done on the loom or after the carpet has been laid flat on the floor. The technique is to cut into the pile along the edge of the pattern, in a slanted direction in order to accentuate the pattern. Subtly graduated shades of color can be separated in this way without having to go to the trouble of weaving an outline for each color.

The Chinese are as famed for their diversity of patterns as they are for the restraint shown in the use of colors. They take their patterns from other decorative crafts including brocade and silk designs, embroideries, bronzes and porcelain. Patterns are not intended as mere decoration, for each of the motifs in a given design has a significant

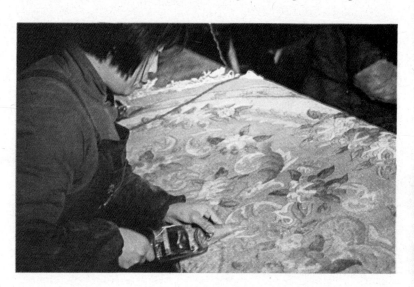

symbolic value based on folklore, mythology and language. Chinese language characters are often found on carpets, and of these the character *shou* meaning "long life" has a special appeal to the Chinese with their reverence for old age. The doubled character *hsi*, often called *shuang hsi*, meaning joy, is an emblem of wedded bliss and was found on carpets given as wedding presents.

Highly stylized mountain and water motifs are common designs on carpets for it is believed that the purest pleasure on earth is to be found on quiet mountains and hills and on drifting water. Mountains and water symbolize luck and long life, as in this poem.

> "Good luck – like the waters
>   of the Eastern sea
>   that are in endless flow.
> Long life – as the pine trees
>   of the southern hills
>   that never aged, grow."   Chinese good luck poem

Calm waters appear as masses of multicolored semicircles, rough water as squarish or triangular shapes topped with dots suggesting spray. And mountains are portrayed emerging from the water.

Until after the Revolution, human beings were rarely depicted on

Workmen wear face masks while shearing the carpets to prevent inhaling the wool fibers.

Workers at Tientsin take a break, their finished carpets glowing luxuriantly all around them.

Left: A stylized sea borders a modern silk carpet.

Above: After embossing, the finished carpets are washed.

Real and mythical creatures have long been popular as motifs. Above, the phoenix and the peacock in a garden of delight, and right, two lively Fo dogs playing with a ball all magnificently depicted on silk carpets.

carpets. There are also five animals which are never shown on carpets: the snake, the scorpion, centipede, frog and lizard. These are called the Five Noxious Animals, and were thought to turn into mischievous spirits that would torment the owner of the carpet.

As in all their decorative crafts, the Chinese dragon holds a unique place. A special kind of carpet, the pillar rug, uses the dragon motif to clever advantage. Pillar rugs are long and narrow and as the name suggests, are used to decorate pillars in palaces and monasteries on festive occasions. When the carpet is laid flat on the ground, the coils of the dragon make no sense, yet when the carpet is wound around the pillar the whole design becomes coherent and the dragon becomes expressive. Pillar rugs are usually made in pairs and for this reason they were favorite gifts, as the Chinese prefer to give their gifts in twos. It is considered impolite to give one of anything.

The phoenix or *feng huang*, another common motif, is not to be confused with the apocalyptic Greek beast. The Chinese phoenix is a mythical animal adorned with everything that is beautiful in birds. It is said to resemble a swan from the front and to have the throat of a swallow, the bill of a fowl, the forehead of a crane, the crown of a mandarin duck. It is also said to have the stripes of a dragon, the neck of a snake and the vaulted back of a tortoise.

Fo dogs, resembling lions more than dogs, have an important place in carpets for they are considered to be guardians and were the companions of the Buddha. Sometimes they are shown in pairs, the male playing with a ball and the female with a pup beneath her paw.

Three floral patterns predominate in carpets: the lotus, chrysanthemum and peony. The lotus is a symbol of summer, for that is when its leaves appear above the water, and of purity because it is able to rise above the muddy waters. It can be distinguished in carpet motifs from chrysanthemums, symbol of autumn and long life, by the lotus seed pods that accompany it. Peonies are regarded as the queen of flowers and cover carpet borders in profusion. Different flowers are seldom combined on the same rug.

Modern Chinese rugs are today made in four centers: Peking, Shanghai, Tientsin and Chingtao. The range of size, color and design has remained much the same since the Revolution. There are four

Closely woven and durable, Tibetan carpets like the ones made here at the Gyantse factory are famous for their beauty.

basic designs called Self-toned Embossed, Peking, Floral and Aesthetic. The first is characterized by its deeply-clipped design in which the main flowers are cut to a higher pile to give an embossed effect. Peking rugs take as their themes natural scenery and people, though traditional symbols such as the Four Symbols of Gentlemanly Accomplishments, the lute, the chessboard, books of poetry and painted scrolls are also frequent motifs. Bats, butterflies and pine trees occasionally appear on Peking carpets.

The Floral design is based on the Peking design but includes flowers not usually used in traditional designs, such as roses and morning glory. There is no border on this type of carpet and the pile is embossed to create a three-dimensional effect. The Aesthetic design was created in the 1920s and incorporates European design influences, such as full-blown roses and peonies.

Modern carpets are generally made much larger than traditional ones, though the texture has been made finer by the use of more knots per foot. The coloring effect has been improved since the last century by a chemical washing process, which mellows the dye colors and gives them a sheen, though this cannot compete with the effect produced with natural vegetable dyes. These magnificent Chinese carpets are exported all over the world.

A luxurious embossed carpet from modern China.

A machine cuts the pile of the carpet level. The embossing and highlighting of the design will be completed afterward by hand.

CHAPTER 9
FLIGHTS OF COLORFUL FANCY

All over China on the ninth day of the ninth month people used to climb the hills around the town taking with them their finest kites. This is the day of the Festival of Ascending on High, sometimes called the Festival of the Double Nine. On the hills of Foochow as many as 40,000 people assembled when the weather was good for kite flying, and by mid-morning the skies were filled with kites of all shapes and sizes, bird kites, insect kites and demon kites. The town guildsmen often made the most magnificent kites of all. The weavers' guild might be flying an eight-foot long goldfish while the tinkers' guild would struggle with a thirty-foot centipede kite. In order to launch the centipede kite, the participants would all stand on stools, each holding a section of the kite and waiting for the perfect breeze to come along.

This same festival was celebrated all over China though no one is quite sure of its derivation. A favorite story of its origin tells of a certain Huan Ching who lived in the town of Joonan and was a pupil of the magician, Fei Ch'ang Feng. One day the magician warned Huan Ching that all his property and possessions were about to be destroyed by a disaster and he must take himself and his family to the top of the highest mountain. On reaching the summit, he was told that he must wear a bag containing chips of dogwood and sip wine in which were floating chrysanthemum petals. As a reward for faithfully following these instructions he and his family were spared, though all his property was destroyed. The festival commemorates his lucky escape.

Another version says that kites are flown in memory of one Meng Chia of whom it is said that when his hat was blown off at a picnic, he remained quite unconscious of the fact. Whichever is the true story, it is the custom that at the end of the day everyone lets go of his kite, allowing it to fly away. The kites, it is believed, carry away

Flying kites of all shapes and sizes was a pastime enjoyed by adults and children alike in old China.

Opposite: A selection of brightly painted modern paper kites from the People's Republic of China.

Above: Modern Chinese bird kites, with brightly painted plumage, are exported all over the world.

with them all evil, bad luck and ill-health for the rest of the year and so anyone finding the kites must burn them.

Kites have their origins in China, though how they came to be invented is unknown. The idea may have come from the pennons or banners that are flown from cords or flexible rods. Reinforcing these banners with bamboo rods creates a simple kite. Chinese folklore gives an account through an anecdote about a farmer whose hat blew off and soared into the sky, giving him the idea of attaching a cord to the hat to control its flight. Other opinions of how kites were first made abound, from the runaway sails of a ship to the wooden bird said to have been invented by the famous engineer Kungshu Phan in the fourth century B.C. and which is said to have flown for three whole days.

Kites were first used for military purposes in China. In 169 B.C., General Han Hsin, while besieging an enemy palace, flew a kite between his forces and the palace walls, from which he was able to compute the distance to his objective so that a tunnel could be dug under the walls. In the middle of the sixth century A.D., the rebel Hou Ching besieged the town of Nanking, isolating it from loyalist troops. The crown prince of Nanking decided to fly a great number of kites in the sky to signal to the loyalist troops who were waiting some distance from the city. On seeing the kites, Hou Ching's officers believed there was magic afoot and ordered their archers to shoot at the kites. The kites seemed at first to fall to the ground but then suddenly changed into birds and flew away. Perhaps the prince had had the lines of his kites cut to allow the wind to carry kite

As this nineteenth century print shows, kite flying attracted many eager spectators as well as keen and skillful participants.

messages to his army, for, in 1232, kites were actually used for a leaflet raid. At the siege of Khaifeng, the besieging Mongols took many prisoners. The Chinese generals of Khaifeng ordered that kites with messages written on them be flown over the enemy lines. When the kites were flying over the prison compound, the lines were cut and the messages inciting the prisoners to escape fell among them.

Early Chinese kites were often fitted with simple musical instruments which were activated by the wind. These instruments took two forms, the simplest of which is a set of little pan pipes or whistles. The other is a kind of Aeolian harp in which metal strings or thin slivers of bamboo are held tightly across an aperture such as an open gourd or between the ends of a bow.

Before the invention of paper, kites were probably made from cloth and wood. Since they were designed for practical rather than aesthetic purposes, these early kites were mainly built in a simple rectangular shape with three tails hanging from the lower edge. It was not until about the twelfth century that kites came to be used mainly for pleasure in China and it was not long before the most diverse and elaborate designs, decorations and colors could be seen in the skies. The most popular forms were of course birds and flying insects – butterflies, dragonflies and grasshoppers. Not only

What better pastime for a windy day? Boys in nineteenth century China enjoy their favorite sport.

Right: This print shows the paper maker pressing stacks of paper flat. Both rice paper and silk were used as cover materials for kites.

Once aloft, the classic centipede kite is a magnificent sight.

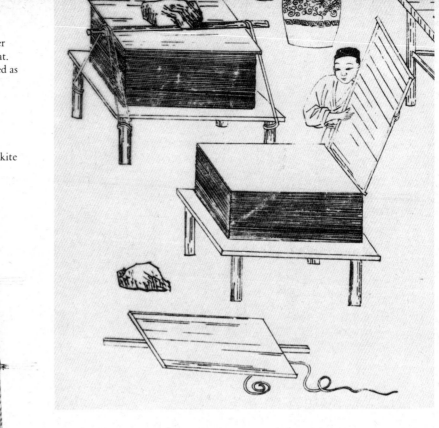

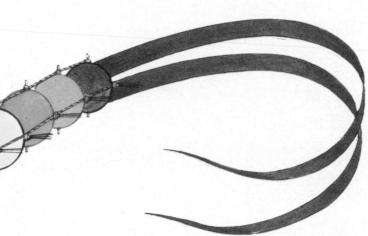

flying creatures were used as kite designs, for the goldfish, carp and tortoise were equally popular motifs.

Simple designs were also used in the making of "fighting kites," for their first function is to be fast and very maneuverable. Kite fighting was a very popular, exciting autumn sport and each contestant would put months into the design and construction of his kite. A long section of the kite line nearest to the kite body is coated with glue and powdered glass. The object of the fight is to cut an opponent's line on the sharp glass line. Contestants would stand fifty feet apart and fly their kites lower than usual in quick swoops. The technique of the fight was to catch an opponent's line and then to try and keep up a sawing motion across his line. It was important, however, to saw faster than the other man for his line, too, was coated with glass. The winner of the fight took possession of his opponent's fallen kite. Each kite was painted with ferocious animals and frightening demons for it was believed that the more terrifying the decoration the better the chance of victory.

One of the most spectacular kites of all, though not the easiest to fly and maneuver, is the centipede kite. The body of the kite, sometimes sixty feet in length, is made of a series of circular bamboo frames covered with brightly colored paper. The disks are held about one foot apart and facing each other, by two or four parallel lines attached to the edge of the disks. Each disk is made in decreasing size down the length of the body, and the head of the centipede is a particularly large and strong disk, painted with a ferocious face. A bamboo pole is fixed horizontally across the center of each disk and projecting over the edges and colored streamers are then attached to the ends. When in flight the whole kite wriggles like a real centipede.

The uses that the Chinese have made of their kites show as much imagination as the kite designs. Kite fishing, for example, was a cunning method by which to take a greater haul of fish. To avoid disturbing the fish by his presence, the fisherman would tie his fishing line to the tail of the kite and allow it to fly some distance out over the water. The gentle movements of the kite, if it was skillfully handled, would cause the bait to appear more lifelike to the fish, and

Keen kite flyers would often spend weeks making and decorating their splendid kites. Sometimes kites were used while fishing to aid the angler in spotting a catch.

Above, and lower picture opposite:
Fantastic insects, and colorful
butterflies and birds are favorite
designs for modern Chinese kites.

Below: Hung with sheaves of rice,
the Fertility kite was flown over the
rice field, symbolizing a new
independence for the son of the
family.

a tug on the line would be quickly seen by the movement of the kite. Scarecrow kites were used on farms to keep birds away from crops. Firecrackers were attached to the kite tail and they were detonated at intervals by the use of slow burning incense sticks on the fuses.

Rice farmers once used kites in fertility ceremonies. When a land-owner's son came of age he was presented with rice paddies of his own and a rice or fertility kite. This was a special kite with a sheaf of unthreshed rice tied to the wingtips. The son flew this kite over his new paddies and the wind would shake the grains of rice from the sheaf. If he could keep his kite flying until all the grains had fallen, it was believed that this would ensure good harvests from that time onward.

Kites so large that they could carry a man have been known for centuries in China, though they have usually been used for a sinister purpose. Legend holds that the Emperor Wen Hsuan Ti one day visited the Tower of the Golden Phoenix, in the city of Yeh, to be received into the Buddhist faith. As part of the celebrations he ordered that the condemned prisoners of the town be tied to large bamboo mats and then be forced to leap off the tower using their mats as kites to carry them to earth. The Emperor called this a "liberation of living creatures" and though none of the prisoners survived, he is said to have been highly amused by the spectacle.

Marco Polo may have been the first European to bring back accounts of Chinese kites and he tells an interesting story of how kites were used for fortune telling. If a merchant wished to know how successful the voyage of his cargo ship would be, he would order the ship's crew to construct a large kite to which they would bind a man. Since no sane man would volunteer for the test, a tramp or drunk on the street was usually found for the purpose. If the kite flew straight up into the sky, it was a good omen, but if it refused to fly or crashed, then this was taken to signify that the ship would never finish her voyage.

Kites made in China today are exclusively for export, for the Chinese Government has banned the flying of kites which was considered an idle activity. Nevertheless, those kites that are made are as varied and colorful as their predecessors and are used by Chinese communities all over the world.

The thrills and excitement of kite flying are captured in this charming print from a nineteenth century album.

TRADITIONAL KITES

Chinese kites are traditionally covered with rice paper or silk. Use either of these or a specially made thin, opaque plastic sheet sold in kite shops to be used as a cover material. Paint the kites with a bright, bold design copying the ones given here or others shown in the book. The scallop design on the Hawk kite was made by drawing around a saucer as a template. Use water colors, acrylics or poster paints to decorate the kites. The tails of the kites make them look very beautiful and dramatic in the air. Without a tail to add stability and counteract the movement of the kite, a flat kite will loop and spin uncontrollably. As a rough guide, the tail should be seven times the length of the kite. Make the Hawk kite tail from two long strips of red crepe paper. The Fertility kite has a tail made of crepe paper or lightweight fabric strips tied at regular intervals onto a length of flying line.

The Fertility kite is painted with the Chinese characters for the Order of the Excellent Crop and the Hawk kite is decorated with a bold, stylized design.

Fertility kite

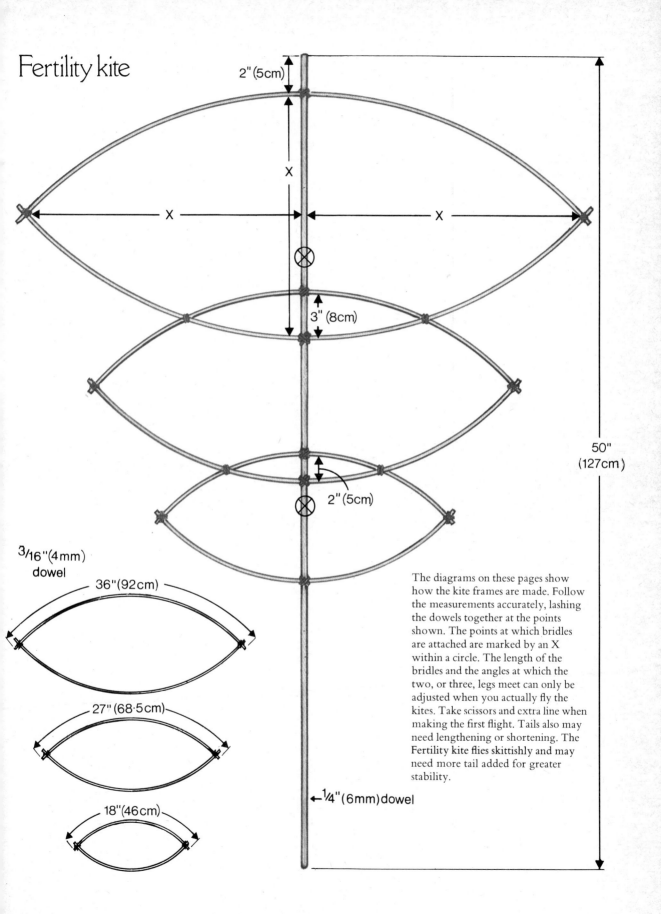

2" (5cm)

X

X

X

⊗

3" (8cm)

2" (5cm)

⊗

50"
(127cm)

3/16"(4mm)
dowel

36" (92cm)

27" (68·5cm)

18" (46cm)

The diagrams on these pages show how the kite frames are made. Follow the measurements accurately, lashing the dowels together at the points shown. The points at which bridles are attached are marked by an X within a circle. The length of the bridles and the angles at which the two, or three, legs meet can only be adjusted when you actually fly the kites. Take scissors and extra line when making the first flight. Tails also may need lengthening or shortening. The Fertility kite flies skittishly and may need more tail added for greater stability.

←1/4"(6mm)dowel

Materials: lengths of dowel 3/16in (4mm) for body section and ¼in (6mm) for centerpole see diagram on page 117, strong linen or carpet thread for tying frames, craft knife, tape measure, scissors, glue, masking tape, cover material, flying line, crepe paper, 2 small metal rings, paints, brush.

A kite must be equally balanced on both sides. After lashing each of the three body sections together, measure both sides to ensure that they are equal. Then mark the center of each stick. Check measurements continually during all stages of kite making.

Hawk kite

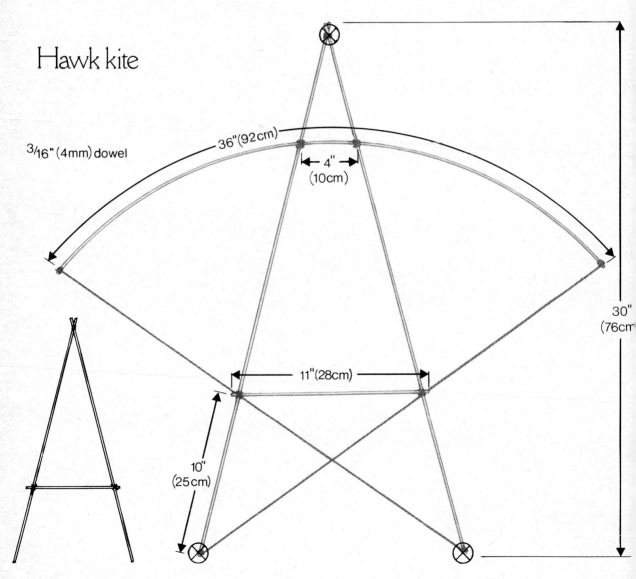

3/16" (4mm) dowel

36"(92cm)

4" (10cm)

30" (76cm)

11"(28cm)

10" (25cm)

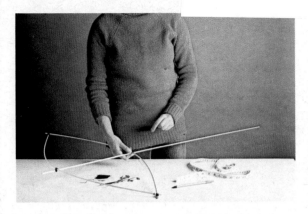

Above: Tie the first body section of the Fertility kite to the centerpole 2in (5cm) from the top. Referring to the diagram on page 117 you will see that each body section should be tied to the centerpole so that it is half as deep as it is wide, indicated by X on the diagram.

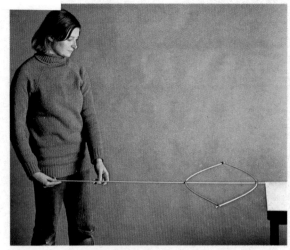

Top right: After attaching each section to the centerpole, check that the frame is equally balanced on both sides by placing top of centerpole on the edge of a table and holding end of centerpole lightly. If the frame remains flat, it is equally balanced. If it tips to one side, then that side is heavier than the other and the lashing must be adjusted. If you have any difficulty bending dowels into the curves required, soak them overnight, then hold the dowel over a gas flame or over steam and gently bend it into a curve.
Below: The diagram on the left shows how to attach the framing lines that run diagonally from wing tips to tail on the Hawk kite. Notch the ends of the stick, lash to prevent splitting and loop and tie framing knots in notch. Center diagram shows most secure method of lashing dowels for kite frame. Use thick cotton or linen thread and wet it before tying. Then, as it dries, it will shrink to make a firm, secure knot. The diagram on the right shows how to tie a bowline knot. This is a very secure knot and should be used for attaching bridles and flying lines to the kites.

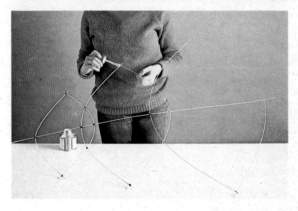

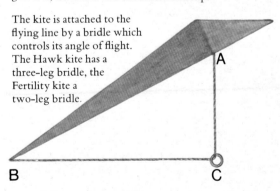

Above: After making a last and final check to be sure of the even balance of the frame, coat all the tied points on the frame with all-purpose glue. This not only makes the knots tighter, it also makes them waterproof so that if the kite gets wet, the knots will not loosen and slip.

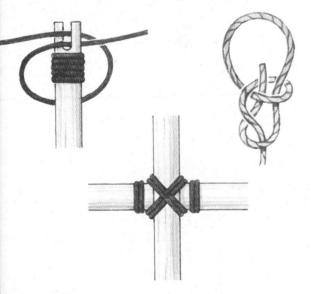

The kite is attached to the flying line by a bridle which controls its angle of flight. The Hawk kite has a three-leg bridle, the Fertility kite a two-leg bridle.

As a guide, cut a length of flying line four times the length of AB. Tie one end at B. Make AC equal to AB and tie a loop or knot on a small metal ring at point C. Holding C straight out, pull AB through lower bridle point until slack is taken up. For the third leg of the Hawk kite cut a length of flying line AC and attach to A and to ring at C. Tie to centerpole. Make final adjustments at time of flying.

To cover the kite frame, lay it section by section on the cover material with the centerpole on the upper side. Hold the frame in place with masking tape. With a felt tip pen, draw around the outside of each body section. Cut out each section individually 1in (2.5cm) outside the drawn line.

To glue the cover, clip all around the edge of cover material up to drawn line. Hold the frame on the cover material with masking tape. Keep centerpole on top so that on the finished kite, it runs along the back. Brush glue on the clipped edge of the cover material and fold excess over the frame.

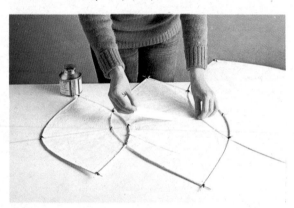

To keep the cover material firmly attached to the kite frame, it must be glued to the centerpole. Cut strips of leftover cover material, spread glue on the centerpole and on either side of it, then cover with the strips. The strips should be similarly glued over exposed sections of the frame on Hawk kite.

Above: Judge the length of the bridle. The bridle should be attached after the kite has been covered and decorated. Tie the bridle to the centerpole, piercing holes through the cover on either side of the centerpole. If the cover material begins to tear, reinforce it with a patch of cover material.

Left: The tail is attached through a hole pierced in the centerpole and the pole is lashed on either side to prevent splitting. The length of the tail should be, on average, seven times the length of the centerpole although this may require adjustment when it comes to flying.

Right: Choose a clear day with a brisk breeze and a site with plenty of open space for launching the kite. Unroll about 70ft (21m) of flying line. Have a friend stand with his back to the wind and hold the kite as high as possible with the tail stretching away directly behind the kite so that it will provide balance as the kite rises into the air. When the kite is released, back up slowly until the kite begins to rise and then unroll more line gradually.

CHAPTER 10
CELEBRATIONS IN PAPER

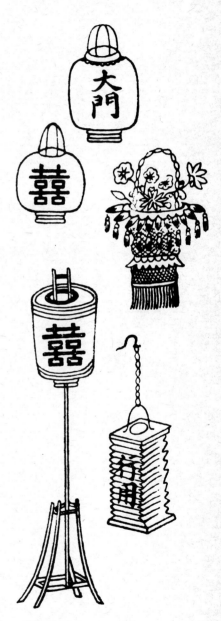

On the evening of the thirtieth day of the twelfth month in the old Chinese calendar, families gathered together around the table where rice wine and simple foods were laid out. Little red lanterns and candles would illuminate the meal, after which incense would be burned on a special table. At eleven o'clock, the streets around would suddenly be filled with the sound of firecrackers and the smell of burning gunpowder, and everyone would rush out to see the display and set off their own firecrackers. Later, families would sleep fully dressed until the sun shone in through their windows and the sound of firecrackers again filled the air to announce New Year's Day.

The Festival of Yuan Tan or New Year was the most important of the many traditional festivals once held in China and is the only one that survives today. Festivals were times of ancestral and religious worship and remembrance but above all they were celebrations of nature and of the people's harmony with nature. Taming nature has never been a part of Chinese philosophy. There is instead a respect for it and a hope that one's efforts and offerings to the forces of nature will yield a good harvest, bring rain at the right time and placate the River God.

Festivals were an intimate part of the old Chinese calendar, which was based on a lunar cycle. The twelve months of the year were further divided into twenty-four *chieh* or "joints" each fifteen days long. The names of the chieh are given according to the characteristic of the particular season; Li Ch'un, the Beginning of Spring, Ching Che, Waking of Insects, Ku Yu, Corn Rain and Shuang Chiang or Frost's Descent. Often, local festivals would take place at the beginning or end of a chieh to offer appeasement or to give thanks for good weather or a plentiful harvest.

The old lunar calendar has now been replaced with the solar calendar we are familiar with in the West, and New Year now falls

This selection of traditional lanterns includes wedding and front door lanterns.

Opposite: Festival days are a good time to stroll in the park and meet friends.

A smiling crowd in holiday mood celebrates May Day in a Peking park gaily bedecked with paper decorations.

on January first, whereas formerly it fell sometime between January twenty-first and February nineteenth. The festival itself has not changed much, except that it now lasts for about three days rather than two weeks, and is combined with the Spring Festival.

Preparations are entered into with great zest and enthusiasm by Chinese families. Homes are spring-cleaned, walls re-papered and doors painted. Little white flour dumplings called *po-po* are eaten by everyone over the whole holiday. Above all, the whole family joins in the making of decorations – little bread dough figures of children and animals which are baked and painted, straw collages, paper and silk flowers and little red lanterns made of waxed paper. Congratulatory messages are written on strips of red paper and pasted on doors. The strips now take the place of the old "door gods," which were said to have originated when the Emperor T'ai Tsung during the T'ang Dynasty was once disturbed at night by spirits and demons shouting outside his door. His General, Ch'in Shu Pao and another man offered to stand guard outside the Emperor's room. In the morning, the Emperor, though pleased that he had had a good night's sleep, pointed out that his two loyal servants had not had any sleep and ordered that in future two paintings of men in battle armor be placed on either side of the palace door. Thereafter he was never disturbed again, and a similar custom was observed by all Chinese households.

One of the most delightful decorations that families make for New

Each province has its favorite paper cut designs. Landscapes come from Kwangtung, theatrical characters from Hopeh and nature motifs from both the Kiangsi and Chekiang provinces.

Year are paper cuts, intricate, delicate patterns cut from tissue-thin paper. These are pasted to the newly papered walls, in the corners of the ceilings and on door lintels. They are also a favorite decoration for lanterns, mirrors, fans and even for the fish served on New Year's Day. They are often stuck to windows and for this reason in northern China they are called *huang-hua*, or "window flowers."

No one knows the origin of paper cuts, though the earliest mention of them is in the T'ang Dynasty, when the Emperor, during the Spring Festival, gave each of his guests a silk flag decorated with paper cuts in the shape of flowers or Chinese characters. Throughout

At the Hungku district Children's Palace near Shanghai youngsters spend an after-school recreation period making and coloring paper cuts.

Customers in a Shanghai paper store browse through selections of colorful paper, choosing their favorites for making the paper cuts and other paper decorations used in festivals.

history frequent mention has been made of paper cuts used as patterns for embroidery.

The craft of paper cuts has usually been the task of the women and girls in a family, and at one time in Shantung Province, a young girl had to learn both embroidery and paper cutting before she married. The paper cuts she prepared for her marriage ceremony were often used to judge her character and how suitable she was for the marriage. Peasant families once made them to supplement their income at the time of the New Year's festivities. The head of the family would do the cutting and the women and children would paint them.

Two techniques are used, one to make scissor cuts and one to produce knife cuts. In the first, a pattern is first cut from thin cardboard and pasted to a pile of, say, ten sheets of very thin paper stitched together with thread. Alternatively, the pattern is fastened to a piece of white paper which is dampened and held over the smoke from an oil lamp. The white silhouette on the blackened paper is then used as the pattern. It is important to use extremely sharp scissors to cut the design.

Knife cuts are more difficult to do but up to seventy sheets can be cut at one time. The sheets are placed in a wooden frame and rest on a base of flexible resin to keep them in place. A sketch of the design is laid on top and the whole is fastened down with nails or pins. The expert craftsman uses many different knives depending on the shape and area he has to cut out. Most of the knives have double-edged blades which vary in shape from rounded to long and pointed. Gouges and punches are also used to help complete the cuts.

The paper cuts are painted, while they are still in the frame, using a brush and a special dye that soaks through the sheets. It is important when using more than one color that the dye does not spread and often each craftsman will have his own secret recipe for a nonspreading dye, which is usually alcohol-based. The amount of alcohol present determines how far the dye will spread, and some craftsmen use distilled rice wine for this purpose.

Each province has its own favorite designs for paper cuts. Kiangsi and Chekiang provinces are known for their motifs inspired by nature; stag, deer, hare and butterflies are often depicted among bamboo groves. Whole landscapes are the themes of paper cuts from Kwangtung Province, while from Hopei come the favorite characters of the theater, the Monkey King and the Lady White Snake and the many other figures of folk tales and mythology. Fatshan City is the center for paper cuts made in silver and gold paper, producing rich and colorful outlines of peonies, the phoenix and court ladies. The most delicate of the flower paper cuts come from Kiangsu Province where they are also used as embroidery patterns, and from Honan come paper cuts for the ceiling, called Ceiling Flowers.

New Year's Day is a time to visit friends and relatives and to wander the crowded streets and parks. Everywhere there are festoons of paper flowers and streamers across the streets, and the delicious aroma of pork buns and spring rolls being cooked in the open air. In the parks, there are theater groups giving displays of songs and dances, and audiences gather around the puppet theaters. There are lanterns everywhere, for no festival would be complete without them.

Above: May Day in Peking.

The nineteenth century print below shows the shop of the New Year ornaments maker.

Above: An intent audience watches an acrobatic display, one of the many attractions of the annual May Day celebrations.

Above right: Dressed in their best and carrying bright, festive decorations, children enjoy the holiday.

Lanterns once played a prominent role in the social and religious life of the people, and though their symbolic significance is no longer recognized, they are still profusely used for decoration. Lanterns were once given as gifts, particularly for weddings, for they symbolized the principle of light or Yang. Farmers hung them in their fields at harvest time to ward off bad spirits, and there was even a Lantern Festival held from the thirteenth to the seventeenth of the first month of the year. This festival seems to have originated from

Lanterns are still an important part of all Chinese festivals although they no longer play a religious role.

Pu-Qua, an artist of the late eighteenth century, faithfully recorded this lantern maker at work.

Children in Yung Hung kindergarten, in Wuhan, enjoy their performance as much as the audience.

an ancient ceremony to welcome the increasing light and warmth of the sun after the cold of winter. The simplest lanterns are made from split bamboo frames covered with waxed paper colored black, red or yellow. Red is the most common color for it is the color of joy and festivity. The shapes of lanterns seems endless; ball-shaped, square, oblong, octagonal or made in the shapes of animals. Some were once constructed to roll on the ground while the light still burned. Others have a freely revolving fixture inside the lantern which is rotated by the hot air from the light. These lanterns are called *tsou ma teng*, or "pacing horse lanterns" because the revolving figures were often made to represent warriors on horseback chasing each other.

In old Peking there was once a famous Street of Lanterns. There, artisans who had been in the trade for generations supplied every imaginable type of lantern. There were lanterns of silk, sometimes richly embroidered, others of colored glass or of thin white silk on which historical scenes, figures or characters were brightly painted. The more elaborate and expensive lanterns were hung with silk tassels and pieces of carved jade. Most of the traditional lanterns are still made in Soochow, Hangchow and Foochow, including the more elaborate ones which today are hung in public buildings, streets and parks. A pleasant custom no longer practiced today took place on the fifteenth day of the seventh month, when from twilight onward young boys would make lanterns of lotus leaves, by placing candles in the deep hollow of the leaf. The whole leaf would then

A student in Shanghai carefully pastes multicolored tissue paper over a wire frame to create a splendid rooster lantern.

glow a beautiful green and the boys would carry the lanterns through the streets singing,

"Lotus-leaf candles! Lotus-leaf candles!
Today you are lighted. Tomorrow thrown away!"

The custom came down from the Yuan Dynasty, though no one quite knows its origin.

Until not too many years ago the Dragon Boat Festival was a very popular and exciting occasion, particularly in southern China. The festival came on the fifth day of the fifth month and was the occasion for the dragon boat races. In Canton, these races used to last for several days. Thousands of people would crowd the shore and families picnicked on the decks of brightly painted junks. Small

The lantern shop in the nineteenth century print below displays lanterns for every occasion, made from painted paper and silk.

boats abounded, all especially decorated for the occasion. As the time approached for the start of the race, the crowd would become quieter and attention would be fixed on the starting line, and particularly the huge dragon boats. These boats were over ninety feet long, rising at each end and shaped like a dragon's head with wide, open mouth and cruel fangs. The slender body of the boat, which held a double row of oarsmen, was decorated to represent the scales of the dragon. A man stood in the bows of each boat and others, among the rowers, waved bright flags and beat gongs and cymbals. When the race began, the gongs sounded even louder and were joined by the shouts and yells of the crowd, which grew louder still as the winning boat reached the finishing line.

The festival dates back at least two thousand years and is said to commemorate how Ch'u Yuan, a famous poet, threw himself into a river to demonstrate his disgust with the emperor of the time. Tradition has it that people thereafter scattered rice upon the water to feed his ghost. Others consider that the festival is a fertility rite which is meant to induce the dragons of the air to struggle together and so cause rain to fall. Another custom at the time of the Dragon Boat Festival was for women to cut small tigers, gourds and clusters of cherries and mulberries from silk gauze and string them on colored

Above: The fireworks maker in this nineteenth century drawing ties fire crackers into elaborate shapes.

Below: Flowers of light blossom over Peking on May Day. Fireworks are an important part of Chinese festivals.

Above: Shapes cut from silk gauze
protected children from demons.
Right: Gigantic riddles, prepared by
schoolchildren, give the May Day
crowd an English lesson.

silk thread. These were fastened to the collars of clothes worn by
small children to protect them from demons.

In modern China the most important holidays in addition to New
Year are May Day, the international workers' day, and National
Day, this latter celebrating the founding of the People's Republic on
October the first, 1949. All over China, people celebrate this anni-
versary and the festivities, which last for two days, are as colorful as
New Year. Like New Year, the streets and parks are crowded with
people in their best clothes and carrying paper flowers. Concerts are
given in the parks and the trees are hung with an abundance of red
lanterns, for red is both the traditional color of joy and the national
color of China. National Day combines the color and frivolity of the
old festivals with the pomp and ceremony of the new China.

Below: Preparation for the May
Day celebrations in the Square of
Heavenly Peace in Peking.

PEASANT PAPER CUTS

Paper cuts are used in China as patterns for embroidery as well as decorations for lanterns, fans and containers. They are often displayed in a window and they are therefore called *huang-hua* or window flowers even if they are not flower motifs.

Fragile, intricate paper cuts are not difficult to make if they are cut out carefully and slowly. To make paper cuts, you will need either a pair of scissors with fine, sharp blades or a craft knife with replaceable blades so that you can change the blade when it gets dull. You can cut a stack of up to ten paper sheets at a time using a craft knife but it is difficult to cut out more than two or three at a time with scissors. Use crisp, lightweight white or colored paper such as tissue paper or drawing paper. First trace the pattern you are copying onto a piece of paper and then staple or stitch around the edges of the sheets with the pattern sheet on top. Begin cutting from the center of the design and work outward cutting the outline last. Cut slowly, turning the stack of paper into the knife or scissor blades when cutting curves. If you are using a craft knife, place the stack on an old wooden board to prevent the paper from slipping during cutting.

Right: Baste the sheets of paper together with the traced outline on top. Place the stack of papers on a wooden board and begin cutting the rooster starting from the center of the design and working outward. Knife blades must be razor sharp, so change them if they become blunt.

A picture of a red cock is often painted on the wall of a house in China in the belief that the rooster will protect against fire.

Above: This bold rooster motif from Shensi Province is a good pattern on which to practice paper cutting.

Stack many colors of paper together so that the rooster will be cut out in many hues.

The bright, clear colors of drawing inks are ideal for painting paper cuts, although you can use poster or water paints if you prefer. The paper cuts may curl up at the edges once they are painted. To flatten them, place them between two sheets of white tissue paper when the paint or ink has dried and leave them overnight under a heavy book. Finished paper cuts can be used to decorate window panes, greeting cards, lampshades and lanterns. Instructions on page 143 show how to make a paper New Year lantern decorated with a selection of colorful paper cuts.

Flowers such as these regularly appear in all Chinese crafts. The lotus, chrysanthemum, flowering plum and peony are particularly popular as representations of the seasons.

Stylized theatrical characters require skillful cutting, whereas cuddly pandas would make delightful decorations for a child's paper lantern.

NEW YEAR LANTERN

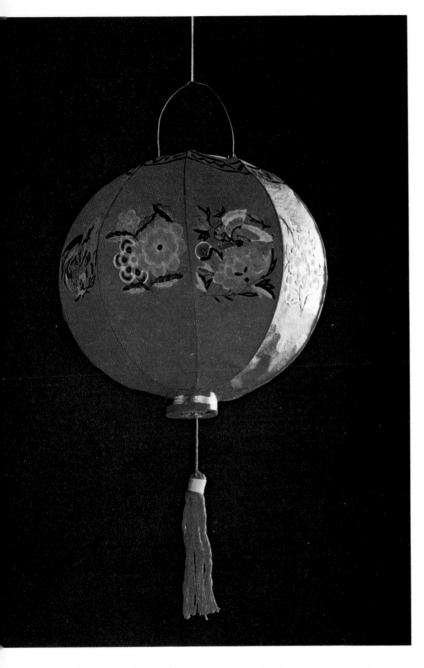

This lantern is decorated with a selection of Chinese paper cuts which are glued onto the paper segments. Alternatively, you can paint on motifs using poster or acrylic paints.

This festive paper lantern is so easy to make that a large number can be made quickly for a party. The lantern is covered with tissue paper, but organdy, light cotton fabric or nylon could also be used. The base of the lantern is a short section of wooden dowel. To make a fitting for the candle, hammer a small headless nail into the center of the dowel after fitting the wire struts of the lantern. The candle can then be pushed down onto the nail. Alternatively place a wad of plastic clay in the center of the dowel base and push the candle down into it. Light the lantern carefully and be sure not to leave a lit lantern unattended.

Materials: 12in (30cm) length of thin split bamboo or cane, short length of 1¾in (4.5cm) dowel for the base, and ½in (12mm) dowel for the tassel, coil of thin galvanized wire or florists' wire, fine string, tissue paper, skein each of scarlet and yellow embroidery floss, Chinese paper cuts, quick drying epoxy glue, all-purpose glue, old paintbrush, lump of plastic clay, hammer, awl, wire cutters, round nose pliers, two small headless nails, large scissors, small scissors, red and gold enamel paint, paintbrush.

Soak the bamboo or cane in warm water for a few hours. Flex it gently then twist into a ring, overlapping the ends by 1in (2.5cm), tie with string. Shape ring around a mug or cup.

Cut eight lengths of wire from the coil. If you cannot buy a coil, cut straight lengths and curve them all together around a bowl or any similar rounded object.

Paint the dowel, which will form the base of the lantern, red and gold. Mark into eighths as shown on page 142, make holes for the wires using the awl and a small hammer.

Hammer a nail into the base of the dowel and bend it over to form a loop for the tassel. Rest the dowel on the plastic clay to form a flat stable base while working.

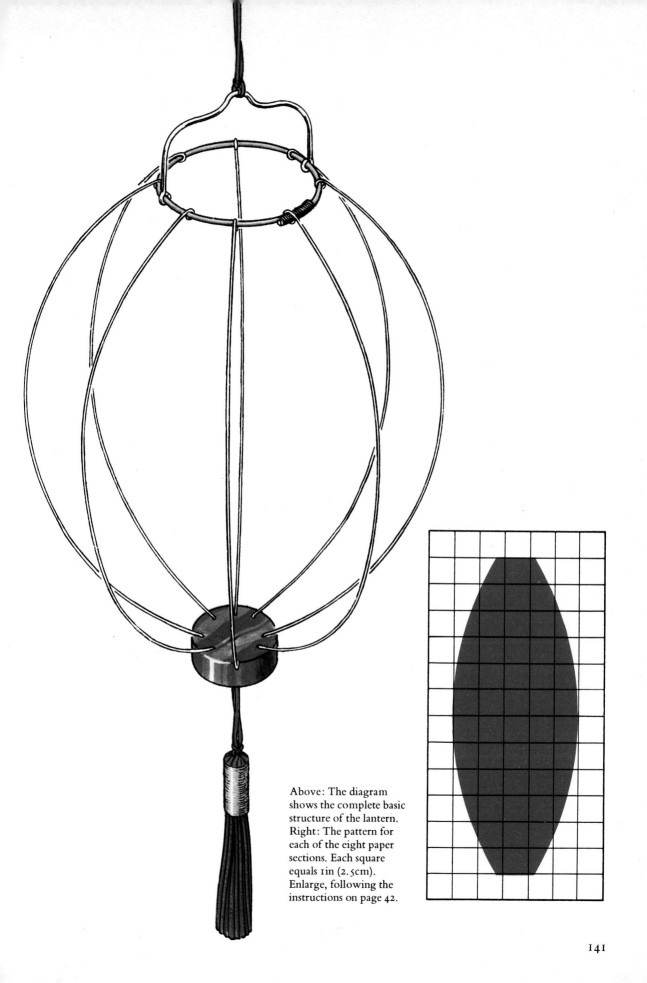

Above: The diagram
shows the complete basic
structure of the lantern.
Right: The pattern for
each of the eight paper
sections. Each square
equals 1in (2.5cm).
Enlarge, following the
instructions on page 42.

Push wires into holes, bend over to edge of dowel, dip in epoxy glue and re-insert. Leave glue to dry. Knock a headless nail into center of dowel to hold candle.

Mark bamboo ring into eighths and twist wires over it. Fix wires in opposite pairs. Check balance and shape of frame after attaching each pair of wires.

Make sure the wire frame is evenly spaced all around. Make a paper pattern for the lantern cover, place on a stack of eight sheets of tissue paper and cut out.

When all the wires have been twisted around the bamboo ring, examine the wire frame from all sides to ensure that it looks evenly balanced and all the wires are equal distances apart. A pattern for the eight tissue paper sections is given on the previous page. The paper sections should be cut large enough so that there is a generous excess when they are glued to the lantern frame. This excess makes it easier to fit the paper over the wire frame. It is trimmed away with a pair of scissors as close to the wires as possible after gluing. Mark the dowel base into segments as shown below to make it easier to space the wires evenly.

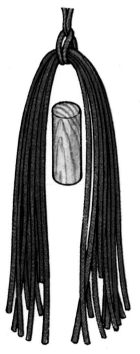

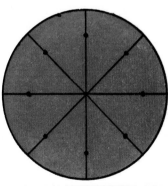

Left: The tassel is very simple to make. Cut a short length of $\frac{1}{2}$in (12mm) dowel. Cut a skein of scarlet embroidery floss into equal lengths of roughly 8in (20cm), tie them together and spread over sides of dowel as shown. Wrap a length of yellow embroidery floss around the dowel, securing the ends with a dab of glue.

Pour some glue into a saucer and with an old paint brush, spread glue over a pair of wires. Starting at the base of the lantern, smooth a sheet of tissue paper over the wires.

Trim the paper at the top and down the sides close to the wires. Fold the edges over the wire. Repeat, covering four alternate sections of the lantern in this way.

The last four sections are covered differently from the first four. Spread glue over a pair of paper covered wires, lay a piece of tissue paper over the wire.

Cover all four sections and allow glue to dry before trimming paper. With small sharp scissors, trim the tissue paper neatly, as close to the wires as possible.

To make the handle, cut a length of wire, loop both ends and fix around the bamboo ring. Round nose pliers will make it easier to bend tight fitting loops in the wire.

Paper cuts make ideal decorations for this lantern. Instructions on page 134 show how to make your own paper cuts in a variety of different designs. Paint on additional details.

Illustrators credits

Marian Appleton pp. 95, 98, 99, 113, 114

Flax & Kingsnorth p. 42

Farhana Khan pp. 16–17, 44–45

Paul Williams pp. 44, 53, 70–71, 104, 112, 117, 118, 119, 134, 136, 141, 142

Photo credits

DATE DUE